Crochet Activity Book

Enjoy Hours of Fun with **100+** Crochet Word Puzzles, Brain Teasers and Picture Activities!

Creative Crochet Themes

Entertaining

Merry Crafters

FUN WITH FIBER

Bonus Number Puzzles!

Large Print

D1709938

Disclaimer

All puzzles, games and activities are designed to heighten your crochet knowledge for entertainment purposes only. The information is as accurate as possible at the time of publication, but errors may occur. Merry Crafters disclaims from any liability for loss if the information contained in the book is used for any other purpose than originally intended.

Copyright

Table of Contents

Section 1
Word Puzzles, Pages 3-50
Word Search, Word Scramble, Word Ladder, Word Find, Logic Puzzle, So Many Words, Trivia, Crossword Puzzle and Cryptogram

Section 2
Picture Puzzles, Pages 51-75
Mazes, Picture This, Odd One Out, Two of a Kind, Reflection, Shadow Match, Last One Standing and Picture Slice

Section 3
BONUS: Number Puzzles, Pages 76-86
Find The Numbers and Sudoku

Section 4
Puzzle Solutions, Pages 87-106

Section 1:
Crochet
Word Puzzles
Challenging Fun!

Classic Wordsearch

Tricky Crosswords

Brain Teasers

Expand Your Crochet Knowledge

Amigurumi Animals & Creatures

Did you know these adorable stuffed toys are a Japanese art form?
Ami, means "crocheted or knitted" and nuigurumi means "stuffed doll".

```
G  I  R  A  F  F  E  N  E  K  C  I  H  C  P
B  I  R  D  D  L  L  O  D  G  A  R  Z  U  D
Y  P  E  A  C  O  C  K  O  R  P  B  P  R  R
T  K  N  C  Q  W  L  R  B  E  L  P  A  U  E
W  H  A  L  E  P  F  L  U  E  Y  G  A  S  P
B  T  N  E  T  T  I  K  N  D  O  S  U  P  R
G  U  N  Q  C  I  B  L  N  N  O  O  H  E  F
P  O  M  A  D  O  G  V  Y  N  M  O  V  E  R
A  Y  L  B  H  R  J  E  I  K  R  A  V  H  X
R  C  M  D  L  P  A  D  R  S  E  H  X  S  O
R  R  O  O  F  E  E  L  E  B  M  I  P  T  F
O  A  N  N  P  I  B  L  A  N  P  P  W  T  N
T  E  K  K  F  I  S  E  E  O  R  P  Z  O  C
N  B  E  E  R  N  G  H  E  I  K  O  P  N  C
N  M  Y  Y  J  K  C  U  D  L  P  A  N  D  A
```

Bear	Dinosaur	Giraffe	Panda
Beaver	Dog	Goldfish	Parrot
Bird	Doll	Hippo	Peacock
Bumblebee	Donkey	Horse	Pig
Bunny	Dragon	Kitten	Puppy
Cat	Duck	Koala	Ragdoll
Chicken	Elephant	Lion	Sheep
Cow	Fox	Monkey	Tiger
Deer	Frog	Mouse	Whale

Crochet Tools

Hidden Message:

Find the words in the grid. When you are done, the unused letters in the grid will spell out a hidden message. Pick them out from left to right, top line to bottom line. Words can go horizontally, vertically and diagonally in all eight directions.

```
S  B  K  O  O  H  T  E  H  C  O  R  C  T  O
R  E  U  R  E  C  R  C  O  C  H  E  T  T  L
E  O  L  T  O  L  S  A  I  N  A  N  P  O  R
D  N  S  D  T  O  J  S  E  C  R  T  O  B  A
N  I  C  G  E  O  R  E  Z  E  K  T  M  L  G
I  B  I  R  E  E  N  U  T  K  G  C  M  C  S
W  E  S  C  G  W  N  T  L  N  T  C  K  T  Q
L  G  S  N  U  Q  A  G  I  E  H  F  E  P  V
L  A  O  K  A  P  Y  D  N  A  R  A  I  D  K
A  R  R  X  G  M  A  R  R  I  M  K  Z  W  K
B  O  S  Y  Z  E  A  T  L  E  N  V  B  R  S
B  T  F  J  B  Y  M  J  R  W  C  R  R  F  C
L  S  N  B  L  O  C  K  I  N  G  M  A  T  Y
R  E  K  R  A  M  H  C  T  I  T  S  Y  D  M
P  O  M  P  O  M  M  A  K  E  R  Q  T  H  T
```

Ball Winder	Pattern
Beading Tool	Pom Pom Maker
Blocking Mat	Ruler
Button	Scissors
Case	Steamer
Chart	Stitch Marker
Crochet Hook	Storage Bin
Darning Needle	Swift
Gauge	Yarn

Solution on page 88

The Magic of Color

What color is on your hook? Do you experiment or stay safe with your color selection? Color theory assists yarn dyers with colorways and designers with color combinations. Choosing the right color can be inspiring.

```
P L P C Y A N R C Y V A N N M
F U Y A R G M A G E N T A R U
N U R D Z D L E G N A R O E S
M L S P N I R G B E I G E D T
N A L C L A R E V L I S V N A
A R N F H E S A P I N K B E R
T O T C E I U R R P E R K V D
B C N L Q A E E L O V H A R
E Y T E A L N B D W B C I L Y
V G R W G A G M N N A L R L P
U Y R O T N O A F E M O A B O
A C M U V J L K P A S L B C F
M Q R I C I D D E E Z R L P K
K A Y D N U G R U B F B U R R
L T M D R T C W H I T E E Q Y
```

Amber	Cream	Magenta	Pink
Aqua	Cyan	Mauve	Purple
Beige	Fuschia	Mint	Red
Black	Gold	Mustard	Rose
Blue	Gray	Natural	Sand
Brown	Green	Navy	Silver
Burgundy	Ivory	Olive	Tan
Copper	Lavender	Orange	Teal
Coral	Lilac	Peach	White

Solution on page 88

Classic Crochet Hat Styles

With so many patterns to choose from, crochet hats are a favorite fall project.
Hats are fun to donate to charity, gift to family & friends, or make for yourself.

```
T  M  V  Z  E  F  L  E  E  H  W  T  R  A  C
B  E  R  E  T  E  R  N  B  U  V  F  S  Q  F
N  L  V  M  I  G  A  U  L  I  Q  A  X  Y  A
E  R  K  N  Z  B  C  R  S  L  I  S  E  W  S
W  C  A  B  R  K  R  O  F  L  U  I  A  R  C
S  E  T  U  E  L  R  E  O  L  P  K  E  C  I
B  B  T  T  P  G  D  R  P  K  A  K  S  V  N
O  C  O  W  B  O  Y  E  R  P  L  P  H  B  A
Y  P  K  A  R  F  I  O  O  A  A  X  Z  O  T
E  Y  R  A  T  L  P  R  T  M  Q  L  P  W  O
H  B  M  A  O  E  I  S  A  L  Y  P  F  L  R
C  S  H  O  Y  B  R  N  I  J  U  L  I  E  T
O  T  C  Z  B  E  A  D  V  B  C  N  Y  R  W
L  A  K  E  E  P  R  Y  A  H  C  U  O  L  S
C  G  D  D  J  T  Q  N  P  A  C  T  A  L  F
```

Aviator	Cowboy	Newsboy
Beanie	Deerstalker	Panama
Beret	Earflap	Pork Pie
Boater	Fascinator	Prayer
Bowler	Fedora	Ribbed
Bucket	Fez	Sailor
Cartwheel	Flapper	Skull
Casque	Flat Cap	Slouch
Cloche	Gatsby	Turban
Coolie	Juliet	Visor

Solution on page 88

Yarn Fibers

Yarn is spun from natural or synthetic fibers. Natural fibers come from plants and animals, while synthetic fibers are man-made. Blends, such as wool and acrylic, have become increasingly popular.

```
N  O  Y  A  R  K  F  T  M  A  C  L  H  R  P
G  P  Y  K  V  I  V  F  C  W  I  D  E  E  L
D  E  L  R  A  M  A  A  T  N  L  K  A  T  X
A  N  G  O  R  A  P  H  E  W  Y  N  T  S  Y
V  K  B  T  V  L  W  N  O  H  R  O  H  E  N
K  E  A  A  A  F  B  O  K  M  C  T  E  Y  Y
O  J  L  Y  M  C  L  R  H  B  A  T  R  L  T
M  R  P  L  A  B  U  R  N  O  M  O  V  O  L
E  K  G  M  I  F  O  O  M  U  X  C  T  P  E
R  L  E  A  X  N  L  O  M  C  S  H  W  M  V
I  L  R  U  N  Y  E  K  D  L  I  Y  E  G  O
N  N  A  P  N  I  T  H  J  E  L  T  E  M  N
O  F  R  J  N  R  C  Y  C  N  K  W  D  Y  P
T  E  R  E  M  H  S  A  C  F  L  E  E  C  E
R  T  M  E  T  A  L  L  I  C  Z  M  C  N  H
```

Acrylic	Faux Fur	Novelty
Alpaca	Fleece	Nylon
Angora	Heather	Organic
Bamboo	Hemp	Polyester
Boucle	Linen	Rayon
Camel	Marled	Silk
Cashmere	Merino	Tweed
Chenille	Metallic	Wool
Cotton	Mohair	Yak

Solution on page 88

What event am I on?

Hidden Message:

Find the words in the grid. When you are done, the unused letters in the grid will spell out a hidden message. Pick them out from left to right, top line to bottom line. Words can go horizontally, vertically and diagonally in all eight directions.

```
A Y A R G N I P P O H S P N D
C M E R O L P X E R A Y A N I
W S A L L H B W D T T R S R S
K N M P D T C T E I F O S E C
T O G S N E N N B C W P T O
R T A Y R U S U S I S E O T U
U T B K F O M I A D V I R A N
N U E T T M S L G E N A T P T
K B T R O R M N N N F E L E S
S F O C D E N T O F E P I E X
H K T R D B S L L P T R T R Q
O P M I R R L E V M S B S F F
W H A N D D Y E D Y A R N Y Y
D E M O N S T R A T I O N K D
T L O C A L Y A R N S H O P S
```

Buttons	Free Pattern	Raffle
Community	Friends	Shopping
Demonstration	Fun	Social Media
Designers	Hand Dyed Yarn	Sponsors
Discounts	Local Yarn Shops	Tote Bag
Events	Map	Trunk Show
Explore	Passport	Website

Solution on page 88

Fabulous Fiber Cruises

Imagine relaxing on a beautiful cruise ship while expanding your crochet skills. What destination would you pick?

```
L L T A D A N A C J L G W C H
N Q F A X B G Y A E N I A M O
E J K D U T N P N F G L B A N
D N D K N S A J R A I L N V G
E P A B E N T A I F M I R N K
W T I E C N N R O R T R G C O
S F I L B C G R I N E I E W N
A L A G E B N L E A D L Q G G
K O W I M I I G A N D I A Z W
S R A U A Y R R A N R H Z N C
A I H M A A T L A R D C P Z D
L D R W N F T L I C E L A N D
A A R I L O L X D E N M A R K
Q O H B C O A U S T R A L I A
N C C S H V T L I J U F X P T
```

Alaska	China	Hong Kong
Argentina	Denmark	Iceland
Australia	England	Ireland
Austria	Florida	Japan
Belgium	France	Maine
California	Fuji	Norway
Canada	Germany	Scotland
Caribbean	Hawaii	Sweden
Chili	Holland	

Popular Crochet Stitches

Learning new crochet stitches can be exciting. Do you prefer in person classes, video tutorials or reading a pattern?

```
G  X  E  N  O  B  G  N  I  R  R  E  H  W  R
G  N  I  K  C  O  L  R  E  T  N  I  I  A  V
E  L  K  N  I  R  C  N  W  N  B  N  T  S  C
G  T  F  M  C  W  R  K  O  V  T  S  E  J  L
T  W  O  R  P  O  F  I  L  E  T  E  E  H  U
S  B  A  C  C  R  L  L  R  G  D  L  B  C  S
O  B  L  P  I  L  I  W  Y  F  B  E  V  T  T
P  T  O  G  U  P  E  B  F  U  M  L  S  A  E
L  P  R  B  C  A  R  D  O  R  O  B  T  H  R
Q  O  B  I  V  H  R  D  E  B  S  B  I  S  R
E  G  O  E  N  F  E  L  Y  S  S  O  T  S  I
K  N  L  P  K  I  N  V  L  G  S  B  C  O  P
I  P  U  F  F  F  T  L  R  E  X  O  H  R  P
P  C  H  A  I  N  N  Y  D  O  H  B  R  C  L
S  H  B  Q  T  R  E  B  L  E  N  S  R  C  E
```

Bobble	Filet	Rib
Bullion	Herringbone	Ripple
Chain	Interlocking	Seed
Chevron	Interweave	Shell
Cluster	Loop	Spike
Crab	Moss	Star
Crinkle	Picot	Treble
Crossed	Popcorn	Trinity
Crosshatch	Post	V Stitch
Double	Puff	

Solution on page 88

Crochet For The Home

Add a touch of charm to your home by decorating with trendy crochet decor.

```
R R T E V I R T W W O L L I P
E E B Y F T C U S H I O N S B
Z N T A D T E A C O Z Y K L T
I I R S T I H H T B Q R A M C
N A C P A H S P C Q N N L R M
A T N S L O M H K A K R T K H
G N A R T A C I C E S H V M B
R O H E R B C R T L W O B O E
O C G W C Z G E H T O H T N D
G L F O B A T H M A T T I M S
G T A L B E V J N A O A H D P
V U G F K K T K E M T T L O R
N Z R S B L D R A R N M W I E
J F A W L F W N U C K T G L A
T B F H T O L C E L B A T Y D
```

Afghan	Container	Pillow
Basket	Curtain	Placemat
Bath Mat	Cushions	Rug
Bath Mitt	Dishcloth	Sachet
Bedspread	Doily	Tablecloth
Blanket	Flowers	Tea Cozy
Bowl	Organizer	Trivet
Coaster	Ottoman	Wreath

Solution on page 88

Famous Crochet Celebrities

Fun Fact: Avid crocheter Kamala Harris is the 49th Vice President of the United States, while Joe Biden is the 46th President. There are periods in history where the two offices were not elected or occupied together.

```
N  Y  W  V  N  V  Y  N  C  Q  B  F  J  X  Z
B  I  R  W  A  T  L  H  P  L  F  M  N  N  K
R  E  A  R  B  N  E  M  K  Q  Q  R  I  L  O
C  E  T  B  E  R  N  N  G  B  M  L  W  A  N
A  N  M  T  O  P  N  A  K  Q  K  G  C  N  A
R  O  M  P  E  C  Y  Q  W  N  K  M  D  N  L
O  M  K  M  L  M  T  T  A  H  R  N  N  O  I
L  Y  G  R  K  J  I  R  A  L  I  M  L  D  M
I  S  N  T  W  D  F  D  U  K  P  T  H  A  A
N  N  R  L  V  A  K  H  L  K  N  Z  E  M  S
E  E  T  C  H  B  E  T  T  E  D  A  V  I  S
R  V  F  T  M  B  B  N  T  Y  R  K  N  K  Y
H  A  E  P  E  E  R  T  S  L  Y  R  E  M  L
E  R  G  N  I  S  S  E  M  A  R  B  E  D  A
A  D  B  E  S  T  E  L  L  E  G  E  T  T  Y
```

Alyssa Milano	Estelle Getty
Aretha Franklin	Katy Perry
Bette Davis	Kurt Cobain
Bette Midler	Madonna
Caroline Rhea	Meryl Streep
Cher	Raven Symone
Debra Messing	Vanna White

Made With Love

Local social service agencies are a great place to donate crocheted items to. Hats, scarves, soap sacks and blankets are always appreciated.

```
K  P  F  D  Y  S  H  E  L  T  E  R  V  T  Y
D  E  R  A  C  R  E  T  S  O  F  W  I  N  R
I  X  E  C  N  R  N  K  J  L  K  F  J  E  T
S  C  T  S  E  C  Q  E  Q  Q  O  R  T  V  F
A  R  N  N  G  R  H  Y  C  R  R  L  M  O  G
S  I  E  A  A  S  H  U  P  I  E  Z  O  C  L
T  S  C  R  G  J  E  N  R  H  P  D  P  E  A
E  I  R  E  N  P  O  E  S  C  P  S  C  L  T
R  S  O  T  I  N  A  L  G  A  H  I  O  X  I
R  C  I  E  G  N  A  N  N  U  L  E  G  H  P
E  E  N  V  A  M  K  T  T  O  F  H  S  R  S
L  N  E  R  I  X  R  K  P  R  F  E  Y  N  O
I  T  S  N  V  Y  B  N  N  Y  J  R  T  H
E  E  A  C  A  N  C  E  R  C  E  N  T  E  R
F  R  N  N  U  R  S  I  N  G  H  O  M  E  K
```

Aging Agency
Animal Shelter
Cancer Center
Churches
Crisis Center
Disaster Relief
Food Pantry
Foster Care
Hospice

Hospital
Nonprofit
Nursing Home
Pantry
Police
Refugees
Senior Center
Shelter
Veterans

Solution on page 89

Flower Embellishments

Beautify a sweater or add pizazz to a hat with a flower embellishment. There are so many crochet flower patterns to choose from.

```
G M D R B A Z A L E A T N D N
Y F A S C E S I T A M E L C B
P L L R U A G A R D E N I A U
P W I E I C L O D I H C R O T
O S D L S G O I N Q R L J L T
P E O T I G O R L I H P A R E
F I F R L K H L C N A C S U R
R N F Y L K F Y D M A B M P C
E O A M Y I S N A R C P I S U
E E D S R I H M N C A Q N K P
S P O I A M E A Y N I Y E R T
I P S D M D T S S N L N E A U
A M H V A I R Y O I O T T L L
M A G N O L I A L R S E G H I
R E D N E V A L Z A G W P F P
```

Amaryllis	Freesia	Marigold
Aster	Gardenia	Myrtle
Azalea	Hyacinth	Orchid
Begonia	Iris	Pansy
Buttercup	Jasmine	Peonies
Carnation	Larkspur	Peony
Clematis	Lavender	Poppy
Crocus	Lilac	Posy
Daffodil	Lily	Rose
Daisy	Magnolia	Tulip

Solution on page 89

Shell, Fan and V Stitches

These beautiful crochet stitches are perfect for a delicate summer shawl,
soft baby blanket edging or a light weight top.

```
Z  O  Y  L  O  O  P  S  N  F  A  N  S  M  L
B  H  T  H  E  L  P  P  A  E  N  I  P  H  L
U  A  K  A  I  T  S  E  L  E  C  Y  C  D  S
N  F  L  C  C  F  O  Y  O  Y  R  T  I  C  E
G  P  M  A  I  I  R  P  L  I  U  L  A  R  Y
A  T  A  S  N  U  L  I  A  D  O  M  X  S  C
L  N  D  H  R  C  Q  E  L  S  I  E  Z  P  H
O  A  E  A  N  I  E  N  D  L  S  Y  U  I  E
W  I  L  D  O  T  L  D  L  O  Y  F  R  L  L
S  D  I  O  G  A  I  A  R  T  F  F  L  U  L
R  A  N  W  A  B  N  T  O  N  A  L  A  T  E
O  R  E  R  R  O  K  A  R  G  Y  L  E  N  S
Y  K  Y  N  D  R  E  E  T  T  E  S  O  R  S
A  N  H  W  M  C  D  K  H  E  L  P  M  I  S
L  E  L  E  G  A  N  T  Y  L  E  T  A  T  S
```

Acrobatic	Elegant	Rosette
Airy	Frilly Fans	Royal
Argyle	Linked	Seychelles
Balanced	Loops N Fans	Shadow
Bungalows	Madeline	Simple
Camilla	Pineapple	Solid
Celestia	Puff	Stately
Delicato	Quick	Tonal
Dragon	Radiant	Tulips
Dutch	Rose	Yo Yo

Vintage Crochet Afghans

From granny squares to patchwork, vintage crochet afghans bring back many fond memories.

```
J F L O W E R J J C A L I C O
G R A N N Y S Q U A R E D F N
R H C T O C S P O H P N C N O
O E K T O M O Q H X O Y A E R
S P D L G J P O W M P S R E V
E R O I A R N Z A V I L T R E
C N E V S E A I R L L H W C H
Y A A T Y E D N E B L E H S C
R N P C S E R D A Y O R E E N
J I O R U A R I S D L I E S M
B M P L I U C I F K A T L E U
B T B P E C E N A T R A T N T
X N C L L S E P A L R G T I U
Z Q F Q T E P T P L G E F H A
R M R A H C L A I N O L O C H
```

Autumn Chevron	Fireside	Lancaster
Blue Diamond	Fleur De Lis	Lollipop
Calico	Flower	Navajo
Caprice	Granada	Ripple
Cartwheel	Granny Square	Rose
Chinese Screen	Heritage	Siesta
Colonial Charm	Honeycomb	Tartan
Colony	Hopscotch	

Solution on page 89

Filet Crochet Motifs

Create patterns, words and interesting pictures with filet crochet. With just two basic stitches, chain and double crochet, a grid is created with open and solid meshes. The results are stunning.

```
L Y L L B U T T E R F L Y R T
E R N I L F A E L R E V O L C
G E G O D F L O W E R S F Q T
N T T I E O W N X L S M D C T
A S X T R P F G X I M T X E K
B O T R X A C F L K M H C L Z
J O B V S H F E A O D E D T E
L R N K I M D F A D L A N I L
N N U C Z R S K E Z L R O C P
G L K Y U D L T C E R T M C P
L E H E R E V R A A N C A R A
N R L I A T A V C L T W I O E
R F B F T T E T U L I P D S N
O V A L S S K C O C A E P S I
K T M R O F R E T T E L R X P
```

Angel	Diamond	Ovals
Birds	Fleur De Lis	Peacock
Butterfly	Flowers	Peony
Cat	Giraffe	Pineapple
Celtic Cross	Heart	Rooster
Chicken	Leaves	Skull
Clover Leaf	Letterform	Star
Daffodil	Oak Leaf	Tulip

        Solution on page 89

Where's my hook?

Sometimes we loose a crochet hook and find it in the most obscure place.

```
B E T W E E N T H E P A G E S
L K N H R B B T E M N N M I E
Y I T H E T C R O C M R R N G
R N E S H I V D H B X A T M D
D T K A T D K P S L E Y S Y I
N H C T U I X L Y Y O N E C R
U E O S B H R M T N I R R F
A P P Y E S M D O L T D M O Y
L R Y M R D N N T Q H E R C M
E O M N E I H D T T E F A H N
H J N I H K N Z X R F F E E I
T E I E W E Q Y E Y L U H T R
N C B J Y H V N T O T T B Z
I T R Z N T G C L C O S N A K
N O I T A C A V N O R V O G N
```

Anywhere But Here

Behind My Ear

Between The Pages

In My Crochet Bag

In My Fridge

In My Pocket

In My Stash

In The Laundry

In The Project

Next To My Shoe

On The Armrest

On The Floor

On Vacation

Stuffed In Yarn

The Kids Hid It

Solution on page 89

Yarn Weights

Using the correct yarn weight, or thickness of yarn, helps achieve the right size and drape of a project. The second step is to check the gauge, or how big the stitches are, with a sample swatch.

```
K G D A E R H T F A R C K L S
F I N G E R I N G L L C B G U
G N T H L R U G D I O K G S P
D V I S U L M K G B L N D U E
E Z N U T L C H W S I M N P R
T S K P C M T E N V O A J E B
S P E E H N B R O M R C L R U
R O L R U A Z R A A U J K F L
O R B C N H K B T F J I N I K
W T U H K G L P U K I U D N Y
T F O U Y F D J M L E N M E N
H L D N N A J K J N K R E B M
G A L K D T H G I L P Y M P O
I C B Y T T H F V T D R M M K
L E W X B B A B Y L N L N P L
```

Afghan	Fine	Rug
Aran	Fingering	Sock
Baby	Jumbo	Sport
Bulky	Lace	Super Bulky
Chunky	Light	Super Chunky
Cobweb	Light DK	Super Fine
Craft	Light Worsted	Thread
DK	Medium	Ultra Fine
Double Knit	Roving	Worsted

Fiber Events

Attending fiber events is a fun way to learn about yarn and the art of crochet. Explore yarn composition through a spinning class, color palettes from an indie dyer or find a new pattern at a meetup group.

```
Z  V  I  R  T  U  A  L  C  L  A  S  S  C  J
M  S  L  A  V  I  T  S  E  F  G  N  R  C  N
G  B  Y  A  R  N  C  R  A  W  L  O  C  P  W
N  R  H  L  X  R  H  T  Y  H  C  W  U  C  O
I  H  U  B  C  M  M  R  T  H  B  O  T  R  H
T  R  Q  O  Q  R  A  B  E  F  R  O  S  O  S
E  H  E  B  T  R  A  T  H  G  P  L  E  C  A
E  L  Z  T  B  R  C  F  Y  L  T  F  F  H  C
M  H  V  I  R  R  E  T  T  N  X  E  N  E  A
D  Q  L  M  U  E  I  B  Q  S  B  S  R  T  P
L  W  L  I  Z  R  A  K  I  N  H  T  A  A  L
I  R  S  Y  A  T  C  T  M  F  N  O  Y  L  A
U  E  L  H  N  W  H  M  S  V  M  W  W  O  L
G  D  C  O  U  N  T  Y  F  A  I  R  G  N  R
L  O  C  A  L  Y  A  R  N  S  H  O  P  G  Y
```

Alpaca Show	Guild Meeting
Charity Group	Library
County Fair	Local Yarn Shop
Craft Show	Retreats
Crochet A Long	Virtual Class
Crochet Cruise	Woolfest
Festivals	Yarn Crawl
Fiber Tour	Yarn Fest

What are you making?

Crochet patterns are plentiful. Do you have a favorite designer, magazine or website? Where do you find the best patterns?

```
Q S N E T T I M N P M W P B T
C C L S S E R D A S U Y N A E
D U G B L S A C H E T R K S P
I K R W A R L A G Y L D S K P
S Q O T D B W M F W O R K E U
H C K E A L Y S A I B E T T P
C R J M D I K B L O U C O Z Y
L R E U Q C N Y O Q R P T O P
O T W T O T E K I O I L H F E
T A E S S T M L R L T C L R T
H H L O K A P X L E N I N A T
L J R C R P O O K O W C E C O
P K Y K A T W C P M M O P S Y
B A B Y B L A N K E T R L O S
R D M N A G I D R A C Y Q F T
```

Afghan	Cozy	Pillow
Applique	Curtain	Poncho
Baby Blanket	Dishcloth	Puppet
Baby Booties	Doily	Purse
Basket	Dress	Sachet
Bookmark	Flower	Scarf
Cardigan	Hat	Shawl
Coaster	Jewelry	Socks
Costume	Mittens	Top
Cowl	Pet Toys	Tote

The Art of Yarn Bombing

June 11th is International Yarn Bombing Day. This is a great opportunity to display knit and crochet items in public by wrapping them around objects (with permission of course). While this street art brings joy to many, be careful not to harm nature.

```
N E E R T E S T A T U E S Y C
Q T M J C R N I L C L M R D B
E N J N S S X A G C M E H P X
P R E B T P M O Y N T L C M W
I F H O I P E C B N S L N O Z
P H O R L R I T A L R A E T R
N L U T A B D L S G I W B O B
I L S B L I P F B L A A R R R
A M E M R B L U E Z H H M C I
R E P M A C S I G E C Q N Y D
D Z K L K L T M N A D M T C G
K F L A G P O L E G R E J L E
E L O P T H G I L M R D R E J
P L A Y G R O U N D R A E Z G
L N X B I K E R A C K Q C N J
```

Bench	Drainpipe	Planter
Bicycle	Fence	Playground
Bike Rack	Flagpole	Railing
Bird Feeder	Garden	Signs
Bridge	House	Statues
Bus	Lamp	Steps
Camper	Light Pole	Stool
Car	Mailbox	Tree
Chair	Motorcycle	Wall

Solution on page 89

Sweet Baby Crochet Gifts

What adorable new baby wouldn't love a soft and cuddly baby blanket!
Handmade crochet baby gifts are perfect for your next baby shower.

```
E  S  D  Z  Y  K  R  G  O  W  N  W  N  F  P
L  K  F  W  S  L  E  E  P  E  R  G  O  N  P
T  C  H  T  O  L  C  P  R  U  B  V  O  H  Y
T  O  C  V  B  L  A  N  K  E  T  N  C  E  E
A  S  E  Y  P  T  X  N  T  J  W  V  O  A  L
R  Y  G  A  B  R  E  P  A  I  D  F  C  D  I
S  P  L  A  Y  M  A  T  R  G  X  Q  M  B  B
P  N  X  J  T  M  S  B  Y  T  I  S  Y  A  O
R  T  E  C  R  S  O  B  T  F  B  D  Y  N  M
A  L  K  T  E  O  E  O  B  I  H  T  R  D  T
G  L  N  R  T  I  Y  N  B  L  S  A  N  A  K
D  A  D  I  S  I  V  N  J  B  O  H  T  M  C
O  B  E  E  L  G  M  E  W  T  W  C  O  T  G
L  S  N  T  T  E  E  T  H  E  R  R  K  E  L
L  O  B  X  P  T  E  P  P  U  P  H  Q  S  S
```

Ball	Diaper Bag	Play Mat
Bibs	Dress	Puppet
Blanket	Gown	Ragdoll
Blocks	Hat	Rattle
Bonnet	Headband	Shoes
Booties	Lovey	Sleeper
Burp Cloth	Mittens	Socks
Cardigan	Mobile	Teether
Cocoon	Onesie	Toy

Flower Power Word Scramble

Flower embellishments add a special touch to crochet projects. Unscramble the letters in each flower to reveal the flower pattern.

1. Y I A S D O

2. P E U C T R B T U

3. A I D D O F L F

4. O A C R A N T N I

5. R D A O M L G I

Word Scramble

Granny Square Projects

HNGAFA   _ _ _ _ _ _

OTLHERPOD   _ _ _ _ _ _ _ _ _

CFRSA   _ _ _ _ _

AJCTKE   _ _ _ _ _ _

PERISPLS   _ _ _ _ _ _ _ _

ASLHW   _ _ _ _ _

ONCOPH   _ _ _ _ _ _

LOLWPI   _ _ _ _ _ _

NGIOTKSC   _ _ _ _ _ _ _ _

MAPL HDSEA   _ _ _ _ _ _ _ _ _

IWNTER THA   _ _ _ _ _ _ _ _ _ _

TAERSCO   _ _ _ _ _ _ _

Word Scramble

Stunning Stitches

NEPEPALPI

_ _ _ _ _ _ _ _ _

RUNAQLEIH

_ _ _ _ _ _ _ _ _

ITLUP

_ _ _ _ _

STHAVRE

_ _ _ _ _ _ _

KFSOOLATR

_ _ _ _ _ _ _ _ _

ENLAIP

_ _ _ _ _ _

OMDIADN

_ _ _ _ _ _ _

RAWOR

_ _ _ _ _

LTEBEHZAI

_ _ _ _ _ _ _ _ _

OCILDORCE

_ _ _ _ _ _ _ _ _

NGRONIEHEBR

_ _ _ _ _ _ _ _ _ _ _

AEKLTNB

_ _ _ _ _ _ _

Solution on page 90

Word Scramble
Scrap Yarn Ideas

MOPPOM   _ _ _ _ _ _

SAELTS   _ _ _ _ _ _

EWYLJRE   _ _ _ _ _ _ _

LSWEFOR   _ _ _ _ _ _ _

SKTEBA   _ _ _ _ _ _

HTOHSCLID   _ _ _ _ _ _ _ _ _

ADMLAAN   _ _ _ _ _ _ _

TESRCOA   _ _ _ _ _ _

TEONMRSAN   _ _ _ _ _ _ _ _ _

EBDHNDAA   _ _ _ _ _ _ _ _

KROMOABK   _ _ _ _ _ _ _ _

ETIVRT   _ _ _ _ _ _

Word Scramble

9 Types of Wool

LPACAA   _ _ _ _ _ _

GRANOA   _ _ _ _ _ _

EMCAL   _ _ _ _ _

SMAEHCER   _ _ _ _ _ _ _ _

OSWLALOBM   _ _ _ _ _ _ _ _ _

TELOMN   _ _ _ _ _ _

ORNEIM   _ _ _ _ _ _

IOARMH   _ _ _ _ _ _

DHTANLSE   _ _ _ _ _ _ _ _

Solution on page 90

Make the Connection

Match the items listed in the two columns by
drawing a line from column 1 to column 2.

Popular Attributes

1. Self Striping

2. Planned Pooling

3. Short Rows

4. Ribbed

5. Chart

6. Top Down

7. Crochet Cable

8. Worked Flat

9. Written Pattern

10. In The Round

11. Construction

12. Design Element

A. Sweater Starting at the Neckline

B. Do Not Finish the Row

C. A Circle of Stitches

D. Creates Stripes as You Crochet

E. Steps to Create a Design

F. Fundamental Aspect of a Design

G. To Assemble or Put Together

H. Specific Design or Color Effect

I. Visual Diagram of Symbols

J. Stretchy Vertical Stripe

K. Texture Added to Fabric

L. Turn Work at End of Each Row

Make the Connection

Match the items listed in the two columns by drawing a line from column 1 to column 2.

Yarn Enthusiast

1. Indie Dyer
2. Spinster
3. Shop Owner
4. Crochet Designer
5. Crochet Instructor
6. Etsy
7. Ravelry
8. Pinterest
9. Instagram
10. Blogger
11. YouTuber
12. Podcaster

A. Produces Audio Recordings
B. Sells Yarn in a Store
C. Writes an Online Journal
D. Small Batch Yarn Dyer
E. Database for Fiber Artist
F. Creates Patterns
G. Produces Video Sharing Website
H. Twists Fiber Into Thread
I. Photo & Video Sharing Network
J. Teaches Classes
K. Online Marketplace
L. Image Sharing & Social Media

Solution on page 91

Make the Connection

Match the items listed in the two columns by drawing a line from column 1 to column 2.

Types of Afghans

1. Graphgan
2. Ripple
3. Mile-A-Minute
4. Corner-To-Corner
5. Round
6. Basket Weave
7. Motif
8. Join-As-You-Go
9. Tunisian
10. Waffle
11. Harlequin
12. Sampler

A. Textured and Squishy Stitch
B. Very Fast to Make
C. Made Up of Many Pieces
D. Made From a Graph
E. Diamond Shape Stitch
F. Has a Circular Shape
G. Zig Zag Pattern
H. Made On a Diagonal
I. Different Motifs Joined Together
J. Emulates a Woven Basket
K. Connect Motifs As You Crochet
L. Forward and Back Pass on Hook

Make the Connection

Match the items listed in the two columns by drawing a line from column 1 to column 2.

Yarn Labels

1. Brand	A.	Batch of Dyed Yarn Identifier
2. Yarn Weight	B.	Thickness of Yarn
3. Gauge	C.	Yarn Length
4. Hook Size	D.	Weight of Yarn Skein
5. Fiber Content	E.	Particular Name of Yarn
6. Yardage	F.	Recommended Tool
7. Yarn Care	G.	Specific Pigment of Yarn
8. Manufacturer	H.	Stitches & Rows Per Inch
9. Lot Number	I.	Composition of Yarn
10. Grams or Ounces	J.	Company That Made Yarn
11. Country of Origin	K.	Washing Instructions
12. Color	L.	Country of Manufacture

Solution on page 92

Word Ladder

Change one letter in each row without changing the order of the letters.

HOOK	LOOP	HANK
____	____	____
____	____	____
COWL	POST	BALL

WOOL	BEAD	SILK
____	____	____
____	____	____
____	____	____
YARD	FINE	TOOL

Word Find

Find the word listed above the puzzle.

LOOM

L	O	M	O	O	M	M	L
O	M	L	M	M	O	O	O
M	L	M	L	O	M	O	M
O	M	L	O	M	L	L	L
M	O	M	M	O	M	O	M
M	O	L	L	M	O	M	L
L	O	O	L	L	M	L	M
O	M	L	O	M	O	M	L

WRAP

W	A	P	R	A	A	P	W
R	P	R	W	P	R	A	P
W	A	A	R	W	A	R	P
P	W	W	P	A	P	A	W
R	A	P	A	R	W	R	A
P	R	W	A	W	P	R	A
A	A	W	R	R	P	A	R
W	P	R	A	A	R	P	P

ARTS

T	R	S	S	A	R	A	T
A	A	R	T	A	S	T	R
S	S	T	S	T	A	A	R
A	T	S	R	A	R	S	T
S	R	T	S	A	T	R	S
A	A	S	T	T	R	S	A
R	S	A	T	R	S	A	R
T	S	S	T	R	A	R	T

ROSE

S	S	O	R	E	E	S	R
E	R	S	S	O	R	R	O
R	O	O	E	S	S	R	E
E	S	E	O	R	O	S	E
S	R	E	S	E	O	R	R
O	R	S	E	S	R	O	R
O	S	O	R	E	R	O	S
R	E	O	S	R	E	O	S

Betty's Crochet Projects - Logic Puzzle

Betty completed several projects for a local charity. Figure out the type of project, color of yarn and how many of each Betty made.

1. Betty made 2 less of the brown item than the blue item.
2. The blanket is either blue or has a quantity of 10.
3. The hats are green.
4. There are 4 more shawls than blankets.

		Quantity				Color			
		4	6	8	10	Green	Brown	Blue	Red
Name	Scarf								
	Hat								
	Shawl								
	Blanket								
Color	Green								
	Brown								
	Blue								
	Red								

Name	Quantity	Color
Scarf		
Hat		
Shawl		
Blanket		

 Solution on page 93

Yarn Project - Logic Puzzle

Four women go to the yarn store and purchase supplies for their new projects. How many skeins of yarn and in which color did each woman purchase?

Clues:

1. Barbara purchased red yarn.
2. Lisa purchased 5 more than the woman who purchased purple yarn.
3. The woman who purchased 5 skeins either bought blue or purple yarn.
4. Joan purchased blue yarn.
5. Joan has 5 more skeins than the woman who purchased green yarn.

		Amount				Color			
		5 skeins	10 skeins	15 skeins	20 skeins	Blue	Red	Purple	Green
Name	Lisa								
	Barbara								
	Wendy								
	Joan								
Color	Blue								
	Red								
	Purple								
	Green								

Name	Amount	Color
Lisa		
Barbara		
Wendy		
Joan		

Solution on page 93

Stitch by Stitch - Logic Puzzle

Each month a group of crocheters gather to stitch together and learn new skills. Classes were taught during the first five months of the year by guest teachers. Each teacher used a new pattern with a unique stitch for their project. None of the projects or stitches were the same. From the information provided can you determine which teacher taught each of the projects, the stitch that was used, and the month the class was held?

1. Connie taught a class on the lap blanket. She taught it exactly one month before the cowl class, which was exactly one month before the crosshatch stitch. Neither Sylvia or Dan taught the crosshatch stitch.

2. The crosshatch stitch was taught at some point before Paula taught a class. Paula did not teach the scarf class.

3. The herringbone stitch was taught after the parquet stitch but at some point before the scallop.

4. The project using the bavarian stitch in March wasn't taught by Sylvia.

5. The hat project wasn't in May and wasn't taught by Kelly.

		Bavarian	Herringbone	Parquet	Scallop	Crosshatch	Hat	Scarf	Cowl	Wrap	Lap Blanket	January	February	March	April	May
		Stitch					**Project**					**Month**				
Teacher	Connie															
	Sylvia															
	Kelly															
	Dan															
	Paula															
Month	January															
	February															
	March															
	April															
	May															
Project	Hat						
	Scarf						
	Cowl						
	Wrap						
	Lap Blanket						

Teacher	Stitch	Project	Month

                    Solution on page 93

So Many Words

Move from letter to letter horizontally, vertically, and diagonally to spell the word in the grid.

How many **SHEEP** can you find?

S	H	E	E	E	S
E	P	E	P	H
E	E	S	E	E
H	H	E	P	E
S	E	E	H	S

How much **FIBER** can you spin?

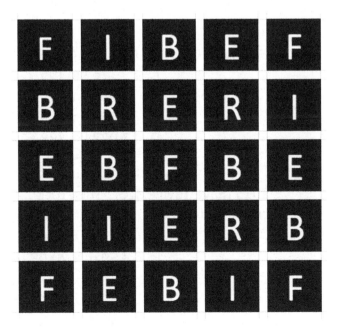

F	I	B	E	F
B	R	E	R	I
E	B	F	B	E
I	I	E	R	B
F	E	B	I	F

Trivia - Crochet World Records

Checkout these and other amazing accomplishments at
https://www.guinnessworldrecords.com, search Crochet

1. On June 25, 2005, Lisa Gentry was awarded the *fastest crocheter* at a Michaels Store (Monroe, LA). How many stitches did Lisa crochet in 30 minutes?
    - A. 3874
    - B. 5118
    - C. 4289
    - D. 6192

2. The *longest crochet chain* was completed on November 26, 2008 by Anne Vanier-Drussel (France). How many kilometers (miles) was the chain when measured?
    - A. 34.66 km (21.54 mi)
    - B. 24.67 km (15.33 mi)
    - C. 60.96 km (37.88 mi)
    - D. 130.00 km (80.78 mi)

3. The *largest crochet hook* was made by Clare and Broa Sams (Colchester, UK) for World Wide Knit in Public Day. On December 11, 2017 the diameter measured 11 cm (4.3 in). How long did the crochet hook measure?
    - A. 2.77 m (9 ft 1 in)
    - B. 2.41 m (7 ft 11 in)
    - C. 3.40 m (11 ft 2 in)
    - D. 3.76 m (12 ft 4 in)

4. On July 29, 2018, 67 Blankets for Nelson Mandela Day (South Africa) created the *longest crocheted scarf* as a tribute to Nelson Mandela. How many kilometers (feet) did the scarf measure?
    - A. 29.176 km (95,722 ft)
    - B. 13.987 km (45,889 ft)
    - C. 38.199 km (125,325 ft)
    - D. 27.028 km (88,675 ft)

5. Caron yarn company showcased the *largest Christmas stocking* on December 8, 2015 (Fayetteville, NC). The stocking was created from over 1,100 knitted and crocheted blankets. How large did the stocking measure?
    - A. 20.52 m x 9.98 m (67 ft 4 in x 32 ft 9 in)
    - B. 48.59 m x 20.09 m (159 ft 5 in x 65 ft 11 in)
    - C. 43.43 m x 22.71 m (142 ft 6 in x 74 ft 6 in)
    - D. 25.76 m x 11.02 m (84 ft 6 in x 36 ft 2 in)

6. Mother India's Crochet Queens (Chennai, India) set a world record for the number of *crocheted Christmas decorations displayed*. How many decorations were counted on September 15, 2019?
    A. 75,864
    B. 59,239
    C. 82,996
    D. 66,158

7. Susie Hewer (UK) achieved 2 records on April 13, 2014. Not only did she beat her own finish time at the Virgin Money London Marathon, she did it while *crocheting the longest chain during a marathon*. What was the length of the crochet chain?
    A. 167.4 m (549 ft 3 in)
    B. 206.7 m (678 ft 2 in)
    C. 139.4 m (457 ft 4 in)
    D. 119.0 m (390 ft 5 in)

8. On April 30, 2017 The Singleton Crafters (New South Wales, Australia) held a community wide crochet event, encouraging new crocheters to participate. How many *simultaneous crocheters* were recorded that day?
    A. 427
    B. 604
    C. 821
    D. 769

9. On January 21, 2018 Mother India's Crochet Queens (India) presented the largest *display of crocheted sculptures*. How many crochet sculptures were on display in Chennai, India?
    A. 58,917
    B. 43,286
    C. 62,893
    D. 29,727

10. The longest crocheting marathon was achieved by two friends on February 6, 2020. How many hours did Jadranka Smiljic and Anita Kac (Slovenj Gradec, Slovenia) crochet for?
    A. 15:10:17 Hour(s):Minute(s):Second(s)
    B. 28:05:00 Hour(s):Minute(s):Second(s)
    C. 24:35:15 Hour(s):Minute(s):Second(s)
    D. 20:12:20 Hour(s):Minute(s):Second(s)

Solution on page 95

Industry Standards

Guidelines Established by Craft Yarn Council for Crochet Uniformity

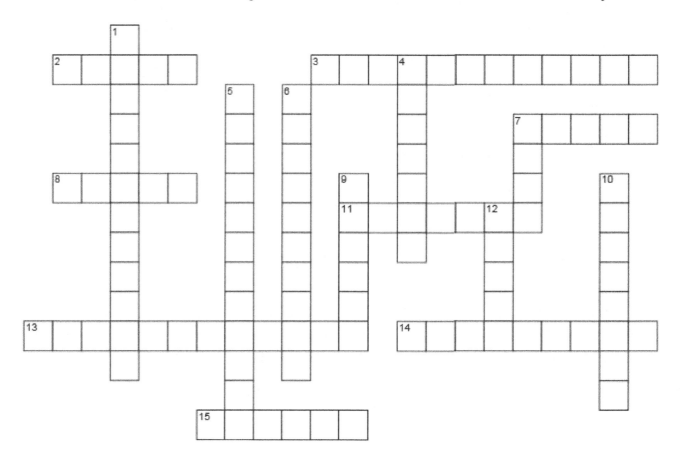

ACROSS

2 Name or trademark used by the manufacturer to identify the yarn

3 Used to identify yarn by weight, hint WPI (3 wds)

7 The appearance of yarn as defined by a light source, such as hue, brightness and saturation.

8 Crochet pattern using symbols

11 Measurement indicating length of yarn in a skein

13 Material yarn is made out of (2 wds)

14 Visual rendering of a project within a pattern

15 Symbol to designate various thicknesses of yarn

DOWN

1 Company Name

4 Project instruction

5 Lace, Sock, Sport, DK, Worsted and Bulky are all examples of this (2 wds)

6 Symbol on a pattern to indicate the complexity of the project (2 wds)

7 Symbol to designate how to clean a finished garment

9 A number that ensures consistent coloring (2 wds)

10 Recommended to obtain the optimal gauge for the yarn weight (2 wds)

12 Optimal measurement obtained using a specific hook and yarn weight

Crochet Idioms

Abbreviations only a crocheter can appreciate.

ACROSS

1 Yarn Acquisition Road Trip
4 Not Crochet Related
5 Mile A Minute
9 In Search Of
12 Pattern Accumulation Beyond Life Expectancy
13 Trashed Object Abandoned In Disgust
14 Projects In Grocery Sacks
15 Projects In Bags
17 Take Along Crochet
19 Unfinished Object
22 Local Yarn Store
23 Crochet Mojo
25 Fresh Off The Hook
26 Yet Another Project
27 Project Half Done
28 Just Off The Hook

DOWN

1 One Who Loves And Collects Yarn
2 Thanks In Advance
3 To Rip Out Your Stitches
6 Must Get Back To Crocheting
7 Work In Very Slow Progress
8 Work In Progress
10 Pattern
11 Join As You Go
16 Special Treasures All Secretly Hidden
18 Crochet Along
19 Unstarted Object
20 Haven't Started Project Yet
21 Hot Off The Hook
23 Crochet In Public
24 Obsessive Crocheting Disorder

Popular Crochet Projects

How many have you made?

ACROSS

3 Embellishment on a hat
4 Soft hat for hair loss (2 wds)
5 Woven storage container
7 Shopping bag
9 Hand covers
12 Stuffed animal
13 Indoor shoe
14 Bed covering
15 Shoulder wrap
17 Baby snuggle sack
18 Decorative feature, ornamentation
21 Blanket or throw
22 Kitchen textile

DOWN

1 Pullover top
2 Sleeveless Garment
4 Jacket with open front
5 Place holder between pages
6 Head covering
8 Clean pots and pans
10 Cleans kitchen surfaces
11 Headrest
13 Holiday item hung on a mantel
16 Cloak with a center hole
19 Neck wrap
20 Closed hooded garment

Solution on page 96

Selling at Craft Shows

Tips & Tricks For Success

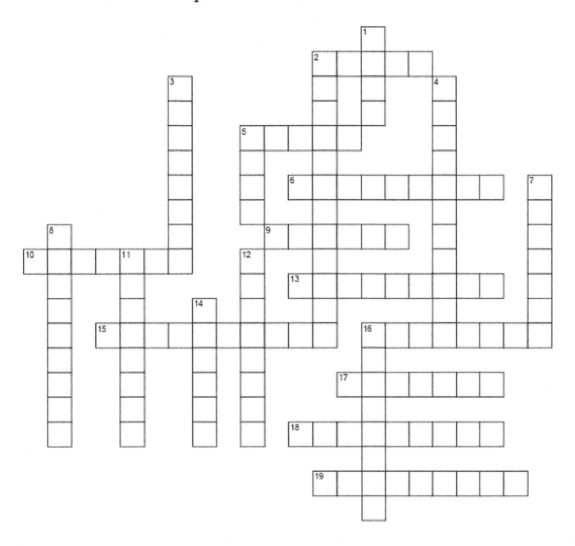

ACROSS

2 Vendor space to set up
5 Type of mailing list that is the least expensive way to advertise
6 Stocking product throughout the day
9 Suggest complementary or similar products
10 Too much of this can be overwhelming to customers
13 Supplies needed to wrap purchases
15 Payment option in addition to cash (2 wds)
16 Process to focus on in advance so ensure success
17 Fixtures, props and tablecloth for the booth
18 Finished product for sale
19 Event where artisans sell goods they have made (2 wds)

DOWN

1 A desired amount of sales to plan your inventory
2 Item given to other people with contact information printed on it (2 wds)
3 Raffle or free item to draw people
4 What you must submit to apply for a craft show
5 Online marketplace to sell handmade items
7 Factor show expenses, material cost, labor, wages and taxes when calculating this
8 Prop used to display garments
11 Cost to be in a craft show (2 wds)
12 Offer this to sell through old inventory or off-season items
14 Allows customers to see how great they look in the item
16 Label each item with this so customers don't have to ask (2 wds)

Solution on page 96

Cryptogram Puzzles

Solve the hidden quote by breaking the code.
A hint for each puzzle is on page 96.

1.

YAO YW DK DYME ONZLELAS MUERQFUK ALSCEM GUM

BRME DO UAF U TYEEVO YW GLAO UAF U ZQYZCOE

TYYJ. -BOMMLZU HUQO

. . . .

2.

EQUCKRXRKW RI RPKUDDRNUPEU YCXRPN

OLP. -CDSUQK URPIKURP

. . . .

3.

L RKKI LTVMC L RKKI. AKJC LTVMC AKJC YE

YLBXMZZ UMHKYMZ HCKHAMV. RQTM LXB LCV

LCM QXZMILCLURM. KRMS

. . . .

4.

WEDWMJY MKF CDELMJX SEDC MDCJFLGZ YD MDY. IKZJY

PJZZJYY NJOOU

. . . .

Cryptogram (Cont.)

5.

HCJZTO QTZCH: S XSON HK KCTD OUCON BCHZ XSUN

TZASFFO. -UCKFMT M'ONZC

. . . .

6.

ROTRKWC UJ NP NRRWJJULFW NOC CKNC RTDWJ ZUCK N

FURWPJW CT LW SOTFUGUR. GONPRUPW CTQMTQ

. . . .

7.

KD CIUY LYILNY ZEKJJYX BEX QUIQGYJYX, JGY

HIUNX HIONX VYY DYHYU HBUV BEX B HGINY NIJ

NYVV UIBX UBPY. NKNT QGKE

. . . .

8.

DZHDXRB MYARL CR PW YWWRZ SRPDR BXPB Y

BZRPLIZR RPDX PWN RARZJ NPJ. GINYBX KRZZRBB

. . . .

Solution on page 97

Cryptogram (Cont.)

9.

DHIPTK LK BN TXVK PZHIELH'U SHZI. -TBVK

CZSHI

. . . .

10.

GDIE YBMNI MVVABI JAWML YBMNI YBNIDVDJNIDAS.

-LIMXENSDM XMNBR-WJXEMM

. . . .

11.

Q JQPM MGWGDJKO DJQZP PKMU VW UJK SVMMKK

UQHPK GDW'U Q TKDD; GU'D QW VHCKSU VM QFU.

-DUKRJQWGK RKQFP-TSRJKK

. . . .

12.

LM ADVHOMP SN LM NWDZUUBMP WV DMIMIFMD.

GW HSN BGCM HSWQLGOU SO MBMJLSOW QDVQLMW. -XSB

IQPMDIGP

. . . .

Cryptogram (Cont.)

13.

QLOG DZBX AZ JZS KXXA WXREAXR O VBZVLXG

HBZFXVG OKA RZDX LZG VZVZO? VLZDHVOUX

. . . .

14.

MNOSB XKWQ MKSNJDS O UKS JW ZKBFDQ GZJGNQS? BQR

JA O BSKSGN

. . . .

15.

KWZJRAXM FT AFSXKXTT. FSWJFYWAFHY RWT YH

WJX. WYB BMXWST WMX NHMXLXM. -PWKA BFTYXV

. . . .

16.

G'OS JIY LIDS IR DN QSLY NBFCL RFID WBFV

QSCUZSL, PBDW WILYL BCE CSXLWBWSF LYBCEL. -I.

ZSCFN

. . . .

17.

OKT NTR YL YJE MQLT QZ YL B WQPHMTA DBEP,

HYYA BPA QMM OYHTOKTE. -NQMMQBW ZKBGTZFTBET

. . . .

18.

RYX HQYHTQ LTTQXUWM VY AYYT, YOQ'Z JQLXV MLO

YOTC DTQQP. -QTWFLDQVJ FWSSQXSLOO

. . . .

19.

LVXOWBYE OYT HVMLXPPBYE XAMWBL COVYP SOP EBQXY

YXZ GXOYBYE WM OTTBYE IBFXV WM GC TBXW. ROWSC

SOYXRX

. . . .

20.

K'D IQNIFE AYFKTS AM YRRQ KT AUR

RCRYF-BYIWARYE AM SKCR AUR UMMP I AYF.

-@QKTHIDIHR

. . . .

Section 2:
Crochet
Picture Puzzles
Entertaining Activities!

Fun Mazes

Two of a Kind

Odd One Out

Picture Slice

Relax with Inspirational Puzzles

Who can get to the yarn first?

Solution on page 98

Shear The Sheep

Merry Crafters Fun With Fiber   53

Burr, it's cold!

Solution on page 98

Cute Toys to Crochet

Stitch Your Way Through The Maze

Solution on page 99

Crocheters Love Mandalas!

Solution on page 99

Help Wind The Yarn Ball

Amazing Sweaters

Puzzle Blankets

Solution on page 99

Project Tools

Merry Crafters Fun With Fiber

Picture This #1

Which 3 images are in all 4 boxes?

Solution on page 100

Picture This #2

Which 3 project bags are in all 4 boxes?

Solution on page 100

Odd One Out #1

Which picture is not like the others? Identify 3 differences.

Solution on page 100

Odd One Out #2

Which picture is not like the others? Identify 3 differences.

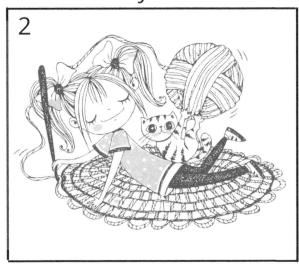

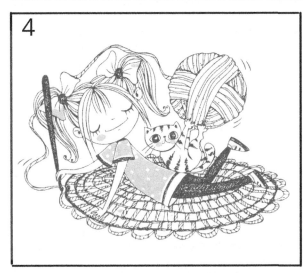

Solution on page 100

Two of a Kind #1

Which two pictures match perfectly?

Two of a Kind #2
Which two pictures match perfectly?

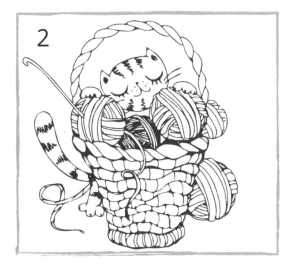

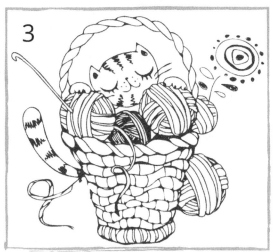

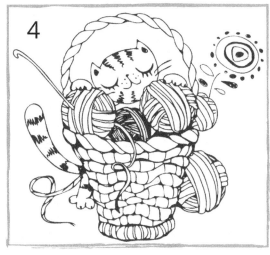

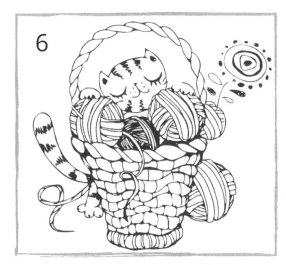

Reflection #1

Can you spot 8 differences in the reflection?

Reflection #2

Can you spot 8 differences in the reflection?

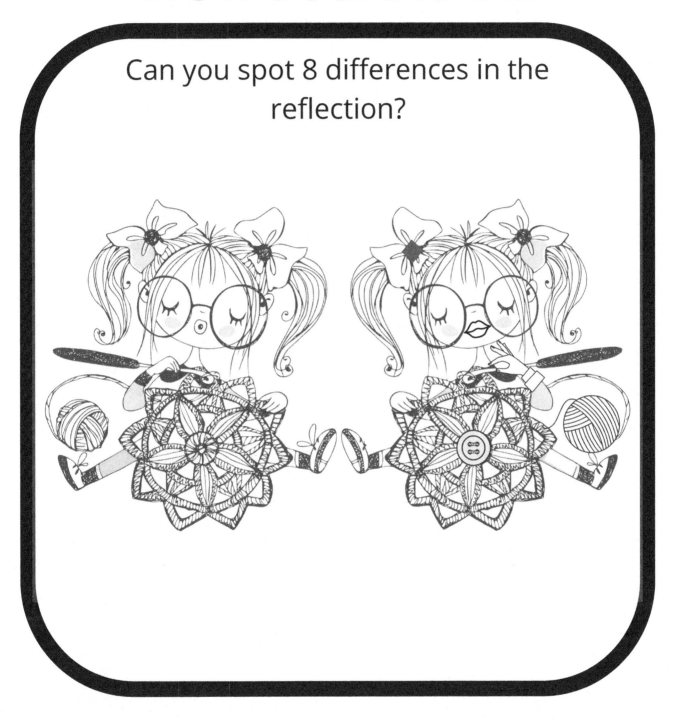

Shadow Match #1

Which shadow matches the picture?

Shadow Match #2

Which shadow matches the picture?

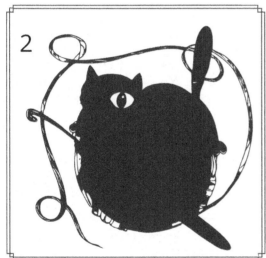

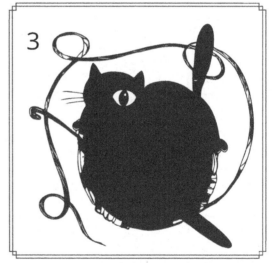

Shining Stars

Cross off all stars above hearts, to the left of triangles,
and between two squares (horizontally or vertically).
How many stars remain?

Winter Projects

Cross off all mittens to the left of scarf, to the right of hat,
and between two sweaters (horizontally or vertically).
How many mittens remain?

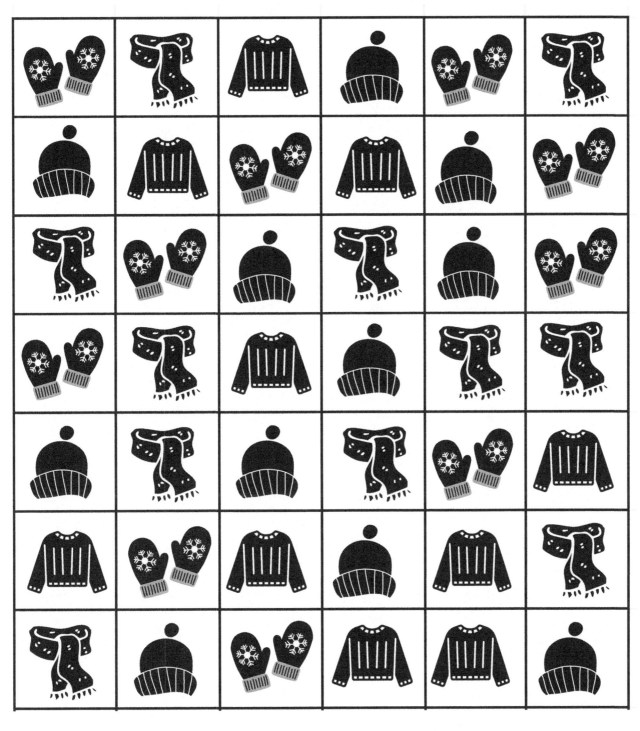

Picture Slice #1

Draw each small square image to create the picture.

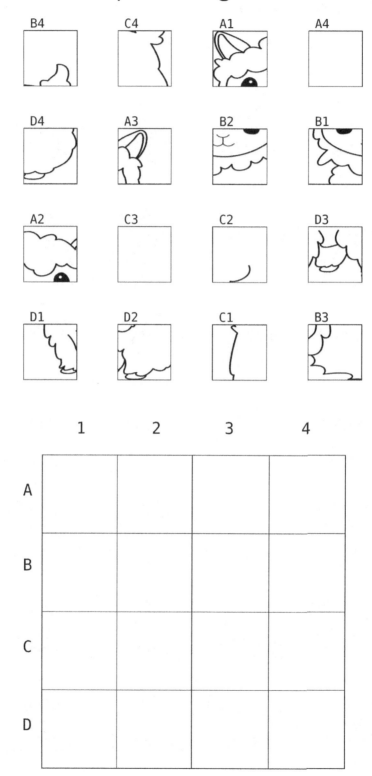

Solution on page 102

Picture Slice #2

Draw each small square image to create the picture.

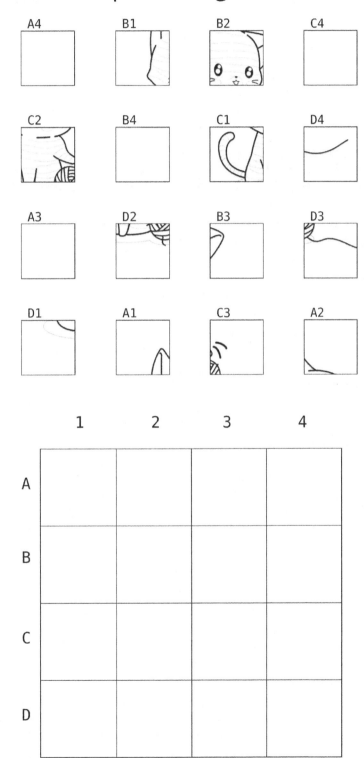

Section 3:

Bonus
Number Puzzles

Popular Math Puzzles & Games!

Find The Numbers

Sudoku

Challenge Your Logic Skills

FIND THE NUMBERS

```
8  6  7  3  6  3  8  0  3  0  1  4  5  8  9
0  7  5  0  7  0  8  0  8  1  8  3  6  1  3
6  8  4  9  5  8  5  7  0  0  4  0  0  8  4
2  5  4  3  5  9  5  3  0  3  4  7  7  0  1
8  3  5  6  0  8  8  9  0  4  1  2  4  7  0
0  2  7  2  3  2  8  3  2  7  1  0  8  5  4
3  0  6  0  6  8  8  7  6  4  2  8  0  8  8
3  9  2  3  4  3  1  0  8  1  4  4  3  3  2
2  4  1  4  8  1  8  3  8  3  5  3  1  6  8
0  7  2  4  4  1  5  9  3  9  6  5  0  7  2
8  5  5  8  0  6  8  7  0  0  4  3  9  0  2
9  4  0  3  1  2  3  3  0  4  5  9  7  2  8
1  1  2  6  1  1  7  2  4  8  1  4  8  3  3
4  4  7  0  0  7  0  1  0  2  8  5  3  5  6
4  1  9  8  3  4  7  0  4  1  8  3  6  7  5
```

00400	8075836	8031097836
14027	8081836	8033208914
82010	20344836	8347041836
203478	50331836	8541030836
381836	51409836	50708081836
949808	82822836	
5887836	209475414	
7059836	378592443	
7421409	807514073	

FIND THE NUMBERS

6	9	6	6	5	2	2	4	3	3	6	8	7	6	6
7	8	5	1	1	9	8	6	1	0	7	1	9	2	5
5	3	9	3	0	2	0	3	1	7	3	2	2	9	5
2	9	7	8	6	7	2	4	4	0	4	9	2	2	5
8	9	8	5	7	1	0	5	0	2	0	4	4	8	9
1	8	9	1	7	7	2	4	0	0	7	0	7	3	9
1	0	8	3	1	8	0	3	4	3	4	0	0	3	2
3	1	8	4	8	5	2	5	6	1	0	3	7	6	0
6	7	2	7	8	1	0	7	4	4	3	6	6	1	0
4	5	7	6	9	4	5	3	6	8	0	1	4	1	4
6	4	1	5	7	8	2	8	2	3	9	0	4	7	9
9	6	9	6	7	7	0	5	6	6	4	3	9	0	6
2	2	7	0	0	1	0	3	2	7	2	0	7	4	5
8	9	1	0	3	4	1	5	3	3	8	1	7	3	4
6	3	2	2	9	4	4	4	5	8	2	2	0	3	5

97867	8987705	3407403094282
851839	70724382	
2484888	7020314836	
5148714	8330897801	

Solution on page 103

FIND THE NUMBERS

```
0  0  9  2  4  1  0  0  8  2  7  0  5  9  4
6  5  5  8  3  1  0  1  1  0  0  6  3  8  3
4  9  6  5  8  4  3  3  0  9  4  1  1  8  2
5  9  2  2  5  2  8  7  8  2  4  8  4  8  5
2  2  7  4  1  2  7  0  0  2  8  5  1  4  9
2  4  3  8  2  0  1  4  5  2  8  9  0  4  6
2  8  8  8  3  2  7  0  5  3  4  7  8  7  3
4  1  1  8  9  5  2  4  9  3  4  2  2  7  2
0  8  9  3  4  9  8  4  2  3  4  2  0  8  2
7  2  7  0  4  1  0  8  8  0  7  2  8  4  6
6  4  7  4  9  0  3  2  4  3  3  4  2  2  2
7  3  3  0  6  6  3  4  1  8  2  0  9  4  4
0  9  3  4  3  0  2  4  3  5  5  3  1  7  4
1  0  5  9  8  4  2  4  3  1  6  9  7  9  7
2  4  3  1  4  3  9  8  4  3  0  1  0  0  6
```

27034	24350843	243342309474
27041	27828301	243942598114
27054	27898201	
27088	34182094	
38794	34203439	
270594	243248943	
2438201	342489501	
3418408	2435472889	
24207314	243143984301	

Puzzle #4

FIND THE NUMBERS

```
5 3 4 5 0 0 0 7 4 1 7 4 3 3 6
1 3 8 4 8 9 7 0 0 9 0 7 2 8 7
1 6 7 3 7 4 3 6 2 1 4 9 7 4 6
3 8 3 4 4 5 5 0 0 7 4 3 3 6 0
2 3 8 8 9 7 3 1 5 4 3 8 8 4 4
2 4 4 0 4 8 4 4 3 4 5 9 4 5 3
1 0 5 7 9 8 8 3 0 1 1 4 0 4 5
4 5 0 6 7 9 9 0 0 1 2 4 0 8 1
2 8 3 8 3 0 4 0 4 4 4 1 7 9 4
7 3 0 3 7 0 3 4 3 8 1 2 1 4 7
6 6 9 1 5 9 7 3 1 9 3 4 4 3 3
1 9 8 9 1 9 3 3 5 8 3 5 3 8 5
2 0 4 9 7 4 9 4 7 1 0 4 5 1 3
0 1 3 8 3 0 8 0 1 4 8 3 4 3 5
1 3 4 7 7 0 2 5 5 1 3 9 3 7 1
```

3081449
3477033
30801483
34737036
34743041
34770255

38400714
38408894
38424104
38489039
347005544
3471470005

3474145039
38450309843
38464548943
38489700907

FIND THE NUMBERS

4	5	4	0	7	1	8	7	3	8	5	3	3	2	5
4	4	9	4	7	7	0	2	4	5	4	3	3	2	4
2	7	1	2	2	7	0	9	4	7	1	0	0	4	0
1	4	2	8	1	9	6	0	7	2	7	1	1	5	3
8	1	5	4	9	1	3	7	5	9	7	4	4	5	0
2	1	0	3	1	4	1	2	0	5	5	4	3	3	9
0	4	0	4	4	0	7	4	9	3	2	5	0	1	1
7	6	2	8	1	7	2	5	7	8	3	2	5	2	4
7	7	0	3	7	4	7	5	7	3	4	9	4	9	0
8	4	4	0	8	2	7	4	4	4	3	5	4	1	5
8	1	0	8	3	5	0	7	1	1	9	0	6	0	8
7	4	5	6	4	5	3	2	4	3	0	3	3	2	7
8	2	5	6	3	0	6	8	4	4	0	2	8	1	8
1	4	1	1	6	3	8	3	0	7	4	7	5	5	3
1	5	4	3	3	0	1	4	7	4	2	1	2	4	1

20278	670339407
143054	1025410254
4741033	2077887811
20405514	2455472834
34475097	2709471004
82427402	5403091405
110414774	7411467414
270314774	94770245433
540718738	839475749814

Solution on page 104

FIND THE NUMBERS

```
1  9  4  2  8  0  3  5  0  1  1  8  2  1  4
9  5  3  1  3  2  1  5  1  4  3  4  2  5  1
1  2  3  4  1  2  0  7  8  0  3  7  1  4  3
5  3  8  3  2  4  1  1  6  3  8  1  8  7  9
8  2  4  3  4  2  8  0  4  3  2  9  9  6  8
2  2  2  8  1  5  4  4  1  8  3  9  8  0  4
7  1  9  8  9  0  8  2  7  9  3  3  2  3  7
4  1  4  2  4  3  7  2  3  8  3  6  0  8  8
1  4  0  4  8  4  4  0  0  4  6  7  3  2  4
0  7  2  1  0  9  6  1  9  3  3  0  7  4  0
7  8  1  4  3  8  0  7  3  0  2  1  9  1  8
8  8  5  7  8  3  4  2  2  4  3  4  2  3  3
7  4  9  4  7  7  4  1  0  1  2  2  6  2  2
8  3  3  3  4  8  9  0  2  7  4  5  6  5  0
5  5  9  5  5  7  4  2  5  9  3  8  1  0  7
```

10147	1478843	022425034
14836	2422439	37020982
24341	3090701	50118214
57834	03389843	388241474
67014	4760382	547209843
85433	7484114	2431439843
89820	8389801	82741078785
574259	8478408	

FIND THE NUMBERS

```
5  9  8  8  6  4  1  0  2  2  0  2  2  1  6
3  9  8  8  6  4  1  4  4  3  0  6  5  4  2
3  1  1  8  9  0  4  7  9  8  8  6  4  7  0
7  6  3  5  6  0  5  4  1  4  6  8  8  9  6
0  8  8  9  5  4  4  1  2  3  0  5  4  0  8
1  9  0  1  8  3  1  0  6  7  3  3  4  2  8
1  7  1  9  8  8  6  4  1  0  4  3  4  6  9
4  0  4  4  4  9  6  1  4  4  2  3  3  1  7
7  9  6  0  5  7  3  4  7  6  6  6  4  3  0
6  4  8  6  4  6  2  4  1  4  6  8  8  9  9
8  6  8  4  8  3  4  4  1  4  6  8  8  9  4
8  8  9  6  3  3  8  2  0  6  8  8  9  9  5
9  8  8  6  4  1  4  7  9  3  0  1  2  1  3
9  9  2  8  9  8  8  6  4  1  4  7  8  1  5
5  8  2  8  7  4  9  8  8  6  4  7  4  7  5
```

4146889	344146889	20220146889
8206889	644146889	38014688982
011476889	746889478	57474688947
14688982	1874146889	64340146889
40146889	2068897094	
054146889	03974146889	
74688974	8344146889	
184146889	8970946889	

Puzzle #8

FIND THE NUMBERS

```
2  0  9  0  8  9  7  4  5  7  8  2  7  9  4
0  3  4  7  4  6  4  9  0  2  0  9  8  4  3
9  6  2  2  4  3  1  4  5  5  0  2  8  4  1
4  5  9  8  4  1  0  9  0  2  6  9  8  2  3
6  3  6  3  4  5  4  2  7  4  9  6  5  0  5
4  7  3  8  8  1  2  0  9  0  9  4  3  8  2
7  9  5  4  7  2  2  9  2  0  7  0  9  0  2
8  6  5  6  2  0  9  0  2  1  4  8  2  8  2
2  0  2  5  0  9  7  1  9  3  4  8  0  3  8
0  8  3  0  1  0  2  4  3  0  2  7  0  2  3
1  7  1  8  3  5  0  6  4  5  2  6  4  6  8
2  1  3  4  4  0  6  0  1  2  0  7  7  5  7
2  3  6  5  2  1  7  4  9  4  7  9  0  2  1
3  0  2  2  0  9  0  8  9  7  4  5  7  4  7
8  5  6  3  1  0  7  3  4  7  9  0  2  5  4
```

209843	82055413	20908974574
20901489	209014604	20946478201
20905019	209021482	209089745782
20907029	209094382	
20946474	209743701	
20974947	20902148282	

84 Crochet Activity Book   **Solution on page 104**

SUDOKU

Fill-in each box with numbers 1 to 9 without repeating a number in each row, column and nine-box square.

Puzzle #1
EASY

7	2	1			9	4	8	
3	5	8	1	2				
	6				5		1	
	4		7		1			
	1			4	2			7
			6				5	
			4	9		2	7	
9			2				6	8
6		2	5	3				

Puzzle #2
EASY

	9			8				3
				5				
3		6	4	9	1	8	7	
			4	5			2	7
	1							6
2		9	1	7				
7		3				2		9
	6	5			4		1	8
1	8			5	9	3		

Puzzle #3
MEDIUM

3	6		5					
4	1		2		8			
				8			9	1
7		1	6	9			4	8
	8	4			6			
5		6						3
6	4	5			3		2	
						8		
8		2		5				6

Puzzle #4
MEDIUM

					5			1
4			6		1			
	2						3	9
	7	3					9	6
			3	6	1	7		
	9			1	2	4		
8							9	6
3		6	2			7	5	8
	5		8				1	

Puzzle #5
MEDIUM

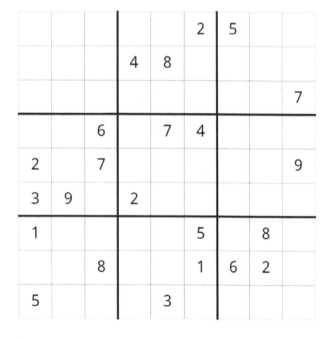

						6	7	
7				5				9
	3	1			6	4	8	
3							6	
	5			6	9		2	3
		2			3	5	1	7
5	6		9					
	8		7			4	2	
								1

Puzzle #6
MEDIUM

		7	9		1		8	
				7		3		
	5				8	2	4	
6			5			1		9
	1	5			9			
2				1	3			4
5	3							
	8		7	5	2		1	
1	7			3			6	

Puzzle #7
HARD

					2	5		
			4	8				
								7
		6		7	4			
2		7						9
3	9		2					
1					5		8	
		8			1	6	2	
5				3				

Puzzle #8
HARD

		8	7					
2			8		4			3
			6		9			
	2		3			6		
1								2
6		5				1		
			5					8
	4	9		2		5		
	7					9		

Solution on page 106

Section 4:
Crochet
Puzzle Solutions

Answers

Clues

Keep Your Brain Young with Challenging Fun Activities!

Word Search

Amigurumi Animals & Creatures

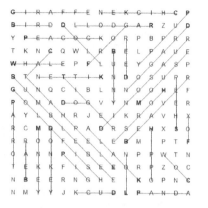

Crochet Tools

Message: Store Crochet Tools In A Project Bag

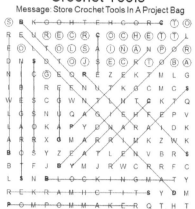

The Magic of Color

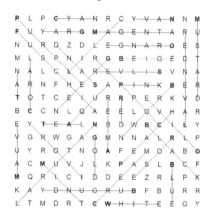

Classic Crochet Hat Styles

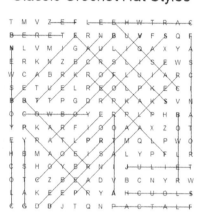

Yarn Fibers

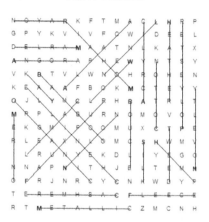

What event am I on?

Message: A Yarn Crawl

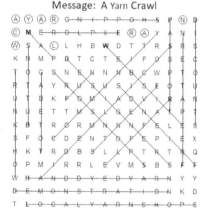

Fabulous Fiber Cruises

Popular Crochet Stitches

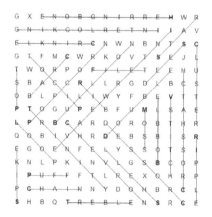

Crochet For The Home

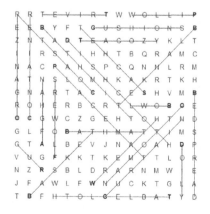

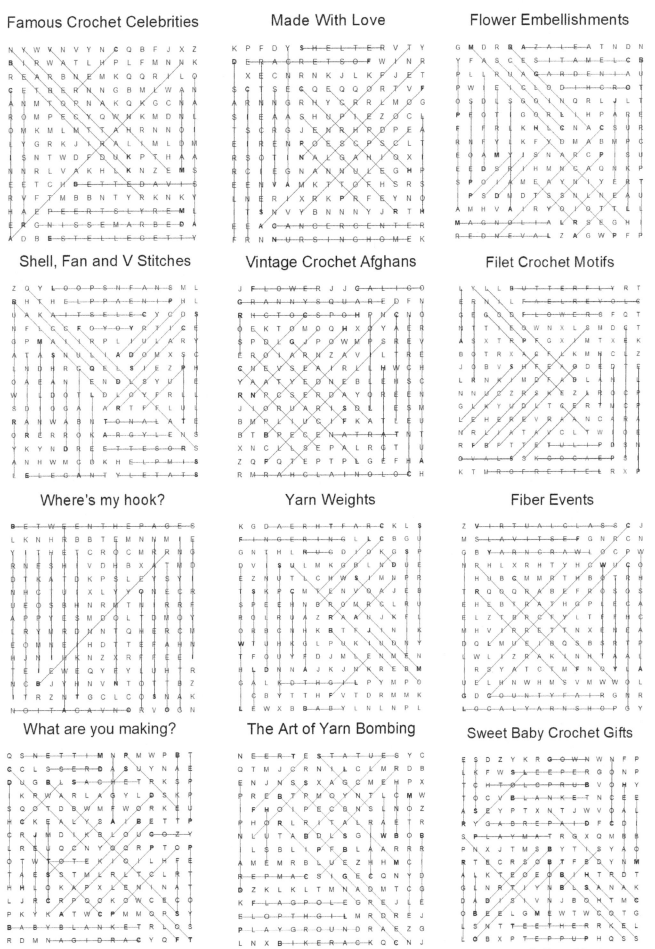

Famous Crochet Celebrities

Made With Love

Flower Embellishments

Shell, Fan and V Stitches

Vintage Crochet Afghans

Filet Crochet Motifs

Where's my hook?

Yarn Weights

Fiber Events

What are you making?

The Art of Yarn Bombing

Sweet Baby Crochet Gifts

Word Scramble

Flower Power: 1-Daisy, 2-Buttercup, 3-Daffodil, 4-Carnation, 5-Marigold

GRANNY SQUARE PROJECTS

HNGAFA	=	AFGHAN
OTLHERPOD	=	POTHOLDER
CFRSA	=	SCARF
AJCTKE	=	JACKET
PERISPLS	=	SLIPPERS
ASLHW	=	SHAWL
ONCOPH	=	PONCHO
LOLWPI	=	PILLOW
NGIOTKSC	=	STOCKING
MAPL HDSEA	=	LAMP SHADE
IWNTER THA	=	WINTER HAT
TAERSCO	=	COASTER

STUNNING STITCHES

NEPEPALPI	=	PINEAPPLE
RUNAQLEIH	=	HARLEQUIN
ITLUP	=	TULIP
STHAVRE	=	HARVEST
KFSOOLATR	=	LARKSFOOT
ENLAIP	=	ALPINE
OMDIADN	=	DIAMOND
RAWOR	=	ARROW
LTEBEHZAI	=	ELIZABETH
OCILDORCE	=	CROCODILE
NGRONIEHEBR	=	HERRINGBONE
AEKLTNB	=	BLANKET

SCRAP YARN IDEAS

MOPPOM	=	POMPOM
SAELTS	=	TASSEL
EWYLJRE	=	JEWELRY
LSWEFOR	=	FLOWERS
SKTEBA	=	BASKET
HTOHSCLID	=	DISHCLOTH
ADMLAAN	=	MANDALA
TESRCOA	=	COASTER
TEONMRSAN	=	ORNAMENTS
EBDHNDAA	=	HEADBAND
KROMOABK	=	BOOKMARK
ETIVRT	=	TRIVET

9 TYPES OF WOOL

LPACAA	=	ALPACA
GRANOA	=	ANGORA
EMCAL	=	CAMEL
SMAEHCER	=	CASHMERE
OSWLALOBM	=	LAMBSWOOL
TELOMN	=	MELTON
ORNEIM	=	MERINO
IOARMH	=	MOHAIR
DHTANLSE	=	SHETLAND

Make the Connection

Popular Attributes

Self Striping	=	Creates Stripes as You Crochet
Planned Pooling	=	Specific Design or Color Effect
Short Rows	=	Do Not Finish the Row
Ribbed	=	Stretchy Vertical Stripe
Chart	=	Visual Diagram of Symbols
Top Down	=	Sweater Starting at the Neckline
Crochet Cable	=	Texture Added to Fabric
Worked Flat	=	Turn Work at End of Each Row
Written Pattern	=	Steps to Create a Design
In The Round	=	A Circle of Stitches
Construction	=	To Assemble or Put Together
Design Element	=	Fundamental Aspect of a Design

Yarn Enthusiast

Indie Dyer	=	Small Batch Yarn Dyer
Spinster	=	Twist Fiber Into Thread
Shop Owner	=	Sell Yarn in a Store
Crochet Designer	=	Creates Patterns
Crochet Instructor	=	Teaches Classes
Etsy	=	Online Marketplace
Ravelry	=	Database for Fiber Artist
Pinterest	=	Image Sharing & Social Media
Instagram	=	Photo & Video Sharing Network
Blogger	=	Writes an Online Journal
Youtuber	=	Produces Video Sharing Website
Podcaster	=	Produces Audio Recordings

Make the Connection

Types of Afghans

Graphgan	= Made From a Graph
Ripple	= Zig Zag Pattern
Mile-A-Minute	= Very Fast to Make
Corner-To-Corner	= Made On a Diagonal
Round	= Has a Circular Shape
Basket Weave	= Emulates a Woven Basket
Motif	= Made Up of Many Pieces
Join-As-You-Go	= Connect Motifs As You Crochet
Tunisian	= Forward and Back Pass on Hook
Waffle	= Textured and Squishy Stitch
Harlequin	= Diamond Shape Stitch
Sampler	= Different Motifs Joined Together

Yarn Labels

Brand	= Particular Name of Yarn
Yarn Weight	= Thickness of Yarn
Gauge	= Stitches & Rows Per Inch
Hook Size	= Recommended Tool
Fiber Content	= Composition of Yarn
Yardage	= Yarn Length
Yarn Care	= Washing Instructions
Manufacturer	= Company That Made Yarn
Lot Number	= Batch of Dyed Yarn Identifier
Grams or Ounces	= Weight of Yarn Skein
Country of Origin	= Country of Manufacture
Color	= Specific Pigment of Yarn

Word Ladder

HOOK	LOOP	HANK	WOOL	BEAD	SILK
COOK	LOOT	BANK	WOOD	BEND	SILL
COOL	LOST	BALK	WORD	FEND	TILL
COWL	POST	BALL	WARD	FIND	TOLL
			YARD	FINE	TOOL

Word Finder

L	O	M	O	O	M	M	L
O	M	L	M	M	O	O	O
M	L	M	L	O	M	O	M
O	M	L	O	M	L	L	L
M	O	M	M	O	M	O	M
M	O	L	L	M	O	M	L
L	O	O	L	L	M	L	M
O	M	L	O	M	O	M	L

W	A	P	R	A	A	P	W
R	P	R	W	P	R	A	P
W	A	A	R	W	A	R	P
P	W	W	P	A	P	A	W
R	A	P	A	R	W	R	A
P	R	W	A	W	P	R	A
A	A	W	R	R	P	A	R
W	P	R	A	A	R	P	P

T	R	S	S	A	R	A	T
A	A	R	T	A	S	T	R
S	S	T	S	T	A	A	R
A	T	S	R	A	R	S	T
S	R	T	S	A	T	R	S
A	A	S	T	T	R	S	A
R	S	A	T	R	S	A	R
T	S	S	T	R	A	R	T

S	S	O	R	E	E	S	R
E	R	S	S	O	R	R	O
R	O	O	E	S	S	R	E
E	S	E	O	R	O	S	E
S	R	E	S	E	O	R	R
O	R	S	E	S	R	O	R
O	S	O	R	E	R	O	S
R	E	O	S	R	E	O	S

Logic Puzzles

Betty's Crochet Projects

Name	Quantity	Color
Scarf	4	Brown
Hat	8	Green
Shawl	10	Red
Blanket	6	Blue

Yarn Project

Name	Amount	Color
Lisa	10	Green
Barbara	20	Red
Wendy	5	Purple
Joan	15	Blue

Stitch by Stitch

Teacher	Stitch	Project	Month
Connie	Herringbone	Lap Blanket	February
Sylvia	Parquet	Hat	January
Kelly	Crosshatch	Scarf	April
Dan	Bavarian	Cowl	March
Paula	Scallop	Wrap	May

So Many Words

So Many Words: How many SHEEP can you find? Answer: 48

S H E E S   S H E E S   S H E E S   S H E E S   S H E E S   S H E E S
E P E P H   E P E P H   E P E P H   E P E P H   E P E P H   E P E P H
E E S E E   E E S E E   E E S E E   E E S E E   E E S E E   E E S E E
H H E P E   H H E P E   H H E P E   H H E P E   H H E P E   H H E P E
S E E H S   S E E H S   S E E H S   S E E H S   S E E H S   S E E H S

S H E E S   S H E E S   S H E E S   S H E E S   S H E E S   S H E E S
E P E P H   E P E P H   E P E P H   E P E P H   E P E P H   E P E P H
E E S E E   E E S E E   E E S E E   E E S E E   E E S E E   E E S E E
H H E P E   H H E P E   H H E P E   H H E P E   H H E P E   H H E P E
S E E H S   S E E H S   S E E H S   S E E H S   S E E H S   S E E H S

S H E E S   S H E E S   S H E E S   S H E E S   S H E E S   S H E E S
E P E P H   E P E P H   E P E P H   E P E P H   E P E P H   E P E P H
E E S E E   E E S E E   E E S E E   E E S E E   E E S E E   E E S E E
H H E P E   H H E P E   H H E P E   H H E P E   H H E P E   H H E P E
S E E H S   S E E H S   S E E H S   S E E H S   S E E H S   S E E H S

S H E E S   S H E E S   S H E E S   S H E E S   S H E E S   S H E E S
E P E P H   E P E P H   E P E P H   E P E P H   E P E P H   E P E P H
E E S E E   E E S E E   E E S E E   E E S E E   E E S E E   E E S E E
H H E P E   H H E P E   H H E P E   H H E P E   H H E P E   H H E P E
S E E H S   S E E H S   S E E H S   S E E H S   S E E H S   S E E H S

S H E E S   S H E E S   S H E E S   S H E E S   S H E E S   S H E E S
E P E P H   E P E P H   E P E P H   E P E P H   E P E P H   E P E P H
E E S E E   E E S E E   E E S E E   E E S E E   E E S E E   E E S E E
H H E P E   H H E P E   H H E P E   H H E P E   H H E P E   H H E P E
S E E H S   S E E H S   S E E H S   S E E H S   S E E H S   S E E H S

S H E E S   S H E E S   S H E E S   S H E E S   S H E E S   S H E E S
E P E P H   E P E P H   E P E P H   E P E P H   E P E P H   E P E P H
E E S E E   E E S E E   E E S E E   E E S E E   E E S E E   E E S E E
H H E P E   H H E P E   H H E P E   H H E P E   H H E P E   H H E P E
S E E H S   S E E H S   S E E H S   S E E H S   S E E H S   S E E H S

S H E E S   S H E E S   S H E E S   S H E E S   S H E E S   S H E E S
E P E P H   E P E P H   E P E P H   E P E P H   E P E P H   E P E P H
E E S E E   E E S E E   E E S E E   E E S E E   E E S E E   E E S E E
H H E P E   H H E P E   H H E P E   H H E P E   H H E P E   H H E P E
S E E H S   S E E H S   S E E H S   S E E H S   S E E H S   S E E H S

S H E E S   S H E E S   S H E E S   S H E E S   S H E E S   S H E E S
E P E P H   E P E P H   E P E P H   E P E P H   E P E P H   E P E P H
E E S E E   E E S E E   E E S E E   E E S E E   E E S E E   E E S E E
H H E P E   H H E P E   H H E P E   H H E P E   H H E P E   H H E P E
S E E H S   S E E H S   S E E H S   S E E H S   S E E H S   S E E H S

So Many Words

So Many Words: How much FIBER can you spin? Answer: 21

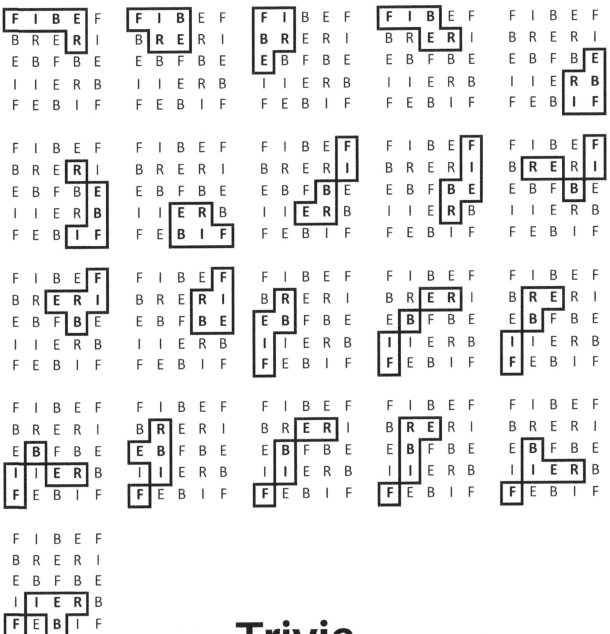

Trivia

Guinness Book of World Records

1-b, 2-d, 3-a, 4-a, 5-c, 6-d, 7-c, 8-b, 9-a, 10-b

Crossword

Industry Standards
Guidelines Established by Craft Yarn Council for Crochet Uniformity

Solution:

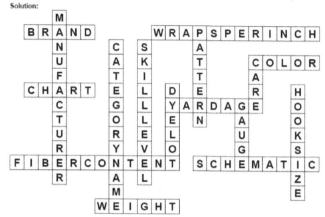

Crochet Idioms
Abbreviations only a crocheter can appreciate.

Solution:

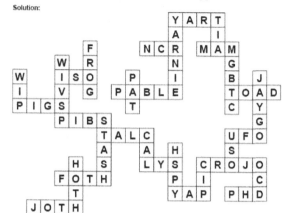

Popular Crochet Projects
How many have you made?

Solution:

Selling at Craft Shows
Tips & Tricks For Success

Solution:

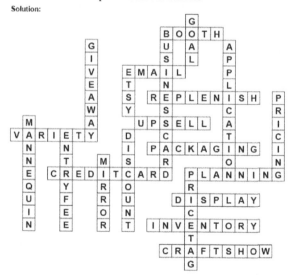

Cryptogram Hints

1: O=E, 2: U=E, 3: L=A, 4: D=O, 5: O=S, 6: U=I, 7: I=O,, 8: P=A,
9: K=E, 10: I=T, 11: Q=A, 12: S=A, 13: X=E, 14: K=I,
15: X=E, 16: S=E, 17: B=A, 18: Y=O, 19: Y=N, 20: A=T

Cryptogram

1. One of my most exciting Saturday nights was just me and a bottle of wine and a crochet book. -Jessica Pare

2. Creativity is intelligence having fun. -Albert Einstein

3. A loop after a loop. Hour after hour my madness becomes crochet. Life and art are inseparable. -Olek

4. Crochet has morphed from homespun to hot. -Janet Bennett Kelly

5. Makers Dream: I wish my yarn stash came with refills. -Taylor O'Shea

6. Crochet is an accessible art that comes with a license to be prolific. -Francine Toukou

7. If more people knitted and crocheted, the world would see fewer wars and a whole lot less road rage. -Lily Chin

8. Crochet gives me an inner peace that I treasure each and every day. -Judith Ferrett

9. Tangle me up like Grandma's yarn. -Luke Bryan

10. With great effort comes great gratification. -Stephanie Pearl-McPhee

11. A half-finished shawl left on the coffee table isn't a mess; it's an object of art. -Stephanie Pearl-McPhee

12. He frowned as he struggled to remember. It was like watching an elephant crochet. -Val McDermid

13. What more do you need besides a crochet project and some hot cocoa? -ChompCake

14. What's life without a bit of risqué crochet? –Sex on a Stitch

15. Laughter is timeless. Imagination has no age. And dreams are forever. -Walt Disney

16. I've got some of my best yarns from park benches, lamp posts and newspaper stands. -O. Henry

17. The web of our life is of a mingled yarn, good and ill together. -William Shakespeare

18. For people allergic to wool, one's heart can only bleed. -Elizabeth Zimmermann

19. Creating and processing exotic yarns has given new meaning to adding fiber to my diet. -Kathy Haneke

20. I'm always trying to reel in the every-crafters to give the hook a try. -@Lindamade

Maze Puzzle

Who can get to the yarn first?

Shear The Sheep

Burr, it's cold!

Cute Toys to Crochet

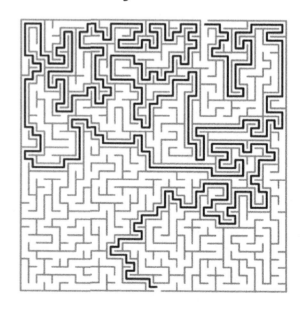

Stitch Your Way Through The Maze

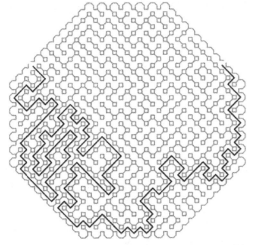

Crocheters Love Mandalas!

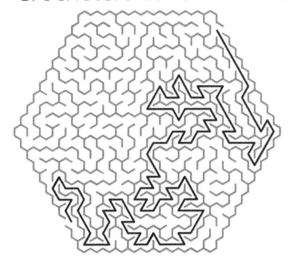

Help Wind The Yarn Ball

Amazing Sweaters

Puzzle Blankets

Project Tools

Picture This #1

Picture This #2

Odd One Out #1

Odd One Out #2

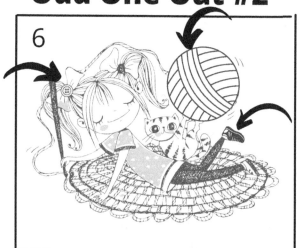

Two of a Kind #1
6 and 7 match

Two of a Kind #2
1 and 4 match

Reflection #1

Reflection #2

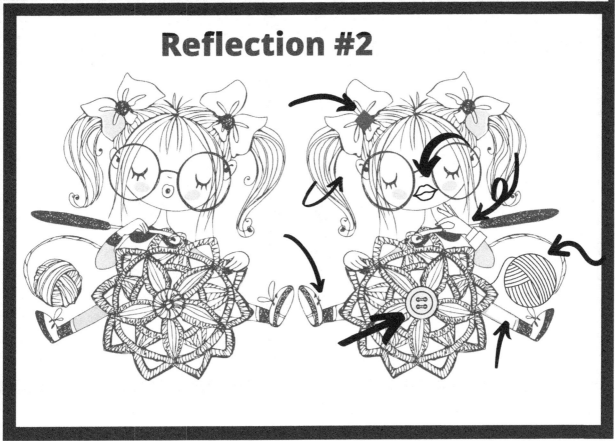

Shadow Match #1

Shadow 2 is a match

Shadow Match #2

Shadow 3 is a match

Shining Stars

1 Star remains

Winter Projects

2 Mittens remain

Picture Slice #1

Picture Slice #2

8		7	3	6	3	8	0	3	0	1	4	5	8
	7	5	0	7	0	8	0	8	1	8	3	6	
		4		5	8		0	0	4	0	0	8	
			3	5	9	5						0	
8	3		6	0	8	8	9	0	4	1	2	4	7
0	2	7	2	3	2	8	3	2			8	5	
3	0	6	0	6	8	8	7	6	4		0	8	8
3	9		3	4	3	1	0	8		4		3	3	2
2	4	1	4	8	1	8	3	8	3		3	1	6	8
0	7		4		1	5	9	3	9	6		0		2
8	5		8	0		8	7	0	0	4		9		2
9	4		3		2		3	0	4	5	9	7		8
1	1		6			7			8	1		8		3
4	4				0	1	0	2	8	5	3		6
		8	3	4	7	0	4	1	8	3	6		

			2								
	8				8						
	9				3		7	3			
	9	7	8	6	7			4	0	4	
8			7					2	0		
1	8	9		7				0	7		
	0	8	3		0			3	4	0	
	8	4	8	5		5		1	0		7
	7	8	1					4	3		
	9	4	5					8	0		
	8	2	8					3	9		
	7	0						6	4		
	1		3					2			
	4			3				8			
							8	2			

	9		4	1			8	2	7	0	5	9	4
		8	3	1	0	1		0					
4			8	4	3	3	0		4				
	9			2	8	7	8	2	4	8			
		7			7	0	0	2	8	5	1		
2	4	3	8	2	0	1	4	5	2	8	9	0	4
			3			5	3	4	7	8	7	3	
4	1	1	8	9	5	2	4	9	3	4	2	2	7	2
		3	4	9	8	4	2	3	4	2			2
	2	7	0	4	1		8	8	0	7	2		
	4	7	4	9	0	3	2	4	3	3	4	2	
		0			3	4	1	8	2	0	9	4	
	9	3	4	3	0	2	4	3					
1	0	5	9	8	4	2	4	3					
2	4	3	1	4	3	9	8	4	3	0	1		

		5	0	0	0	7	4	1	7	4	3	3	
3	8	4	8	9	7	0	0	9	0	7		8	
		3			3						4		
	3	4	4	5	5	0	0	7	4	3	6		
3	8	8	9	7		5			8	4			
	4		4	8	4	4		4		4	5		
	5	7		8	8	3	0		1		0	4	
	0	6	7	9	9	0	0	1		4	0	8	
	3		3	0	4	0	4	4	4		7	9	
	0			0	3	4	3	8	1	2	1	4	
	9			7	3	1	9	3		4	3	3	
	8			3		8			8				
	4			7		0						3	
	3		3	0	8	0	1	4	8	3			
3	4	7	7	0	2	5	5		3				

FIND THE NUMBERS
Puzzle # 5

	5	4	0	7	1	8	7	3	8				5
	4	9	4	7	7	0	2	4	5	4	3	3	4
	7	1		2	7	0	9	4	7	1	0	0	4 0
1	4		8			6		7	2			1	3
	1			9			7	5		7		4	0
2	1	0		1	4		2	0			4	3	9
0	4		4	4	0	7	4	9	3			0	1
7	6	2	8	1	7	2	5	7		3		5	2 4
7	7	0		7	4	7	5	7			9	4	0
8	4	4			2	7	4	4	4			4	5
8	1	0			0	7	1	1	9			0	
7	4	5				2	4	3	0	3			7
8		5				8			0	2	8		
1		1				3				7	5		
1		4	3	3	0	1	4	7	4			2	4

FIND THE NUMBERS
Puzzle # 6

	9	4			0		5	0	1	1	8	2	1	4
	3	1		2			1	4	3	4	2			
	3	4	1	2				0				4		
3		3	2	4		1		3	8		8	7		
8		4	3	4	2	8		4	3		9	9	6	8
2		8	1	5	4	4		8			8	0	4	
7		8	9	0	8	2	7	9	3		2	3	7	
4	1		2		3	7		8		6	0	8	8	
1	4		4	8	4	4	0		4		7		2	4
0	7		1		9		1	9	3		0			0
7	8		4			0		3	0		1			8
8	8	5	7	8	3	4	2		4	3	4			
7	4		4		7	4	1	0	1	2				
8	3		3	4	8	9	0	2	7	4	5			
5			5	7	4	2	5	9	3					

FIND THE NUMBERS
Puzzle # 7

	9	8	8	6	4	1	0	2	2	0	2			
	9	8	8	6	4	1	4	4	3					2
			8			4	7	9	8	8	6	4	7	0
		3		6	0	5	4	1	4	6	8	8	9	6
0	8	8	9			4	4							8
1	9	0		8		1	0							8
1	7	1	9	8	8	6	4	1	0	4	3	4	6	9
4	0	4				6		4	4					7
7	9	6				4		6	6					0
6	4	8				4	1	4	6	8	8	9	9	
8	6	8		8	3	4	4	1	4	6	8	8	9	4
8	8	9			8	2	0	6	8	8	9	9		
9	8	8	6	4	1	4	7	9	3	0	1			
	9	2	8	9	8	8	6	4	1	4	7	8	1	
		8	7	4	9	8	8	6	4	7	4	7	5	

FIND THE NUMBERS
Puzzle # 8

2	0	9	0	8	9	7	4	5	7	8	2	
0		4	7	4	6	4	9	0	2	0	9	8 4 3
9		2			3	1	4	5	5	0	2	8
4		9	8	4	1	0	9	0	2			
6			4			2						
4				1	2	0	9	0	9	4	3	8 2
7				2	2	9	2	0	7	0	9	0 2
8			2	0	9	0	2	1	4	8	2	8 2
2				9		1	9					
0				0		4		0				
1				5		6			2			
				0		0						
				1	7	4	9	4	7	9	0	2
		2	0	9	0	8	9	7	4	5	7	4
			1	0	7	3	4	7	9	0	2	

SUDOKU Solutions

Easy Puzzle #1

7	2	1	3	6	9	4	8	5
3	5	8	1	2	4	7	9	6
4	6	9	8	7	5	3	1	2
8	4	3	7	5	1	6	2	9
5	1	6	9	4	2	8	3	7
2	9	7	6	8	3	1	5	4
1	8	5	4	9	6	2	7	3
9	3	4	2	1	7	5	6	8
6	7	2	5	3	8	9	4	1

Easy Puzzle #2

5	9	4	8	2	7	6	3	1
8	7	1	5	6	3	9	4	2
3	2	6	4	9	1	8	7	5
6	3	8	9	4	5	1	2	7
4	1	7	3	8	2	5	9	6
2	5	9	1	7	6	4	8	3
7	4	3	6	1	8	2	5	9
9	6	5	2	3	4	7	1	8
1	8	2	7	5	9	3	6	4

Medium Puzzle #3

3	6	8	5	1	9	4	7	2
4	1	9	2	3	7	8	6	5
2	5	7	4	8	6	3	9	1
7	3	1	6	9	5	2	4	8
9	8	4	3	2	1	6	5	7
5	2	6	7	4	8	9	1	3
6	4	5	8	7	3	1	2	9
1	7	3	9	6	2	5	8	4
8	9	2	1	5	4	7	3	6

Medium Puzzle #4

7	6	9	3	2	5	8	4	1
4	3	8	6	9	1	5	2	7
5	2	1	4	7	8	6	3	9
1	7	3	5	8	4	2	9	6
2	8	4	9	3	6	1	7	5
6	9	5	7	1	2	4	8	3
8	4	7	1	5	3	9	6	2
3	1	6	2	4	9	7	5	8
9	5	2	8	6	7	3	1	4

Medium Puzzle #5

8	4	5	3	9	1	6	7	2
7	2	6	4	5	8	1	3	9
9	3	1	2	7	6	4	8	5
3	1	8	5	2	7	9	6	4
4	5	7	1	6	9	8	2	3
6	9	2	8	4	3	5	1	7
5	6	3	9	1	2	7	4	8
1	8	9	7	3	4	2	5	6
2	7	4	6	8	5	3	9	1

Medium Puzzle #6

3	2	7	9	4	1	6	8	5
8	6	4	2	7	5	3	9	1
9	5	1	3	6	8	2	4	7
6	4	3	5	8	7	1	2	9
7	1	5	4	2	9	8	3	6
2	9	8	6	1	3	7	5	4
5	3	2	1	9	6	4	7	8
4	8	6	7	5	2	9	1	3
1	7	9	8	3	4	5	6	2

Hard Puzzle #7

7	8	3	1	9	2	5	4	6
6	5	9	4	8	7	2	3	1
4	2	1	5	6	3	8	9	7
8	1	6	9	7	4	3	5	2
2	4	7	3	5	8	1	6	9
3	9	5	2	1	6	4	7	8
1	7	4	6	2	5	9	8	3
9	3	8	7	4	1	6	2	5
5	6	2	8	3	9	7	1	4

Hard Puzzle #8

3	4	8	7	2	5	9	1	6
2	9	6	8	1	4	5	7	3
7	5	1	6	3	9	8	2	4
4	2	9	3	7	1	6	8	5
1	8	3	5	9	6	7	4	2
6	7	5	2	4	8	1	3	9
9	3	2	1	5	7	4	6	8
8	1	4	9	6	2	3	5	7
5	6	7	4	8	3	2	9	1

Made in the USA
Monee, IL
18 December 2021

86239392R00059